GOOD
SERVICE
is
GOOD
BUSINESS

SIMPLE STRATEGIES
FOR SUCCESS

Catherine DeVrye

CAREER
PRESS

Franklin Lakes, NJ

Good Service is Good Business

Cover design by Rob Johnson

Printed in the U.S.A. by Book-mart Press

To order this title, please call toll-free 1-800-CAREER-1 (NJ and Canada:
201-848-0310) to order using VISA or MasterCard, or for further information
on books from Career Press.

**CAREER
PRESS**

The Career Press, Inc.,
3 Tice Road, PO Box 687,
Franklin Lakes, NJ 07417
www.careerpress.com

Library of Congress Cataloging-in-Publication Data

DeVrye, Catherine.
   Good service is good business / by Catherine DeVrye
      p. cm.
   Includes index.
   ISBN 1-56414-556-5 (paper)
   1. Customer services. 2. Success in business. 1. Title

HF54515.5 .D48 2001
658.8—dc21
                                    2001035364

CONTENTS

5 Improve 87

6 Care 99

7 Empowerment 133

ABOUT THE AUTHOR

Catherine DeVrye is a number-one best-selling author and professional speaker and well qualified to comment and write about change and service excellence.

A winner of the prestigious Australian Executive Woman of the Year Award, and frequent media broadcaster, she worked with IBM in sales, marketing, education, and communications. Following a two-year assignment in Japan as Asia Pacific Headquarters Human Resource Manager, she gained a heightened awareness and commitment to quality customer service.

Catherine also has an appreciation of client service in the public sector as a result of eight years with the Victorian Public Service as an adviser to the Ministers of the Department of Consumer Affairs, Education, and Sport. She was involved in the establishment of the award-winning "Life. Be In It" fitness campaign and served as an independent board member of the third largest police service in the world.

As CEO of Junior Achievement Australia, she also acquired an appreciation of the unique challenges associated with the not-for-profit sector. And in her student days, she gained firsthand frontline service experience as a waitress, dishwasher, and cook on an oil rig in Canada and as a computer operator at a bauxite mine in the Outback.

She passionately believes in service to our customers, our community, our country, and our planet, and her personal service was honored by her selection to carry the Olympic torch on the day of the Sydney 2000 Opening Ceremonies.

Catherine holds a master of science degree from Montana and has attended short courses at Harvard University and the Monash Mt. Eliza Business School. A former university lecturer, Catherine has spoken on five continents to a client list of Fortune 500 companies.

Comments on presentations by Catherine DeVrye

Results speak for themselves and here is only a sample of the hundreds of comments from those who have benefited from Catherine's previous books and presentations:

American Express:
"Catherine's easy to read guide about a simple philosophy in business, but very difficult to execute was the official handbook for our teams across our American Express Corporate Travel service delivery teams. It's an excellent reference document, well written and easy to follow to help you stay focused on what's important—your people and your customers."

Australian Customer Service Association:
"As with your clients, our members deserve value. Thank you!"

Australian Institute of Management:
"Participants felt that what they learned would be useful in their own job."

Australian Quality Council:
"An easy-to-read guide about how to build better service-orientated organizations . . . timely and relevant."

Blackmore's Vitamins:
"A jargon-free short read for invaluable long term results-applicable to every organization-large or small-no wonder it's a number 1 best seller!"

Department of Education:
"Your catch phrases echo around the building . . . Down to earth but highly professional . . . I read your book for the fourth time as I always find it encouraging and affirming."

Ernst & Young:
"You gave our client service objectives a great boost . . . thank you for autographing the books as a handy reminder."

Fairfield City Library:
"Being a librarian, I consulted many books on customer service and yours was the only one I devoured from cover to cover . . . based on common sense."

IBM:
"Inspiring and entertaining. Everyone came away with a better idea about service and, more important, what they can do to improve . . . I didn't realize learning could be so much fun."

Kwik Kopy Printing Franchise:
"One of the best presentations on service our franchisees have heard. Your book was a sell-out, with owners also buying copies for staff."

Lend Lease/MLC Insurance:
"Feedback has been nothing short of remarkable. You left financial planners with a clear message that Good Service is Good Business."

Mercedes-Benz:
"We had an all time record year and I am confident you contributed to this."

Monash Mt. Eliza Business School:
"Worthwhile information in an inspiring and entertaining format . . ."

Ray White Real Estate:
"Absolute joy to have a speaker of your caliber upholding the absolute basis of our business—SERVICE, SERVICE, SERVICE!"

Royal Australian Air Force:
"Your model, backed up with humorous analogies helped our quality service . . . doubtful we could have progressed as far without that input."

3M:
"Motivational, uplifting and fun! We went a long way toward achieving our objective of bringing a greater customer service focus to our group."

Tourism Council of Australia:
"Outstanding . . . This is not a standard letter I send but we appreciated the quality of information and positive motivation associated with it."

Westpac Bank:
"You sowed the seed of change . . . The quality program developed from these beginnings will result in a 40-50% improvement in productivity."

Karl Albrecht, author of The Service Advantage and Service America:
"This book by an Australian author clearly demonstrates that service excellence knows no global bounds."

Clarica Insurance:
'Thanks for making my job easier in San Diego. You did everything you said you would do—and more. Your topic was relevant, your presentation dynamic and you received a well-earned standing ovation from the 1000+ audience."

Coca-Cola South Pacific:
"Excellent . . . it was obvious she had researched our company . . . would use again."

International Association Of Business Communicators:
"Attendees in Washington loved your enthusiasm, wit, insight and dynamic speaking style—I'm sure this is no surprise given the lengthy line at your book signing after."

ACKNOWLEDGMENTS

No one else is responsible for this book. I must accept all blame and any possible credit. Hundreds have provided lifetime experiences, upon which some of this text is based.

Thank you to my parents for everything! And Kay, Frank, Grace, and Liz for always being there. Thank you to most of my teachers for providing a thirst for knowledge; especially Dr. Wally Schwank and Helen, who continue to be a source of inspiration as they live life to the fullest in their 80s. Also the Monash Mt. Eliza Business School where I was introduced to the world of business.

Thank you to any employer who ever hired me to wash dishes, make beds, deliver flyers, teach school, be a lifeguard or executive, wait on tables, cook, sell, or whatever; especially Pat Tritter. As much as I hated selling hot dogs, she taught me a lot about loving the customer . . . and others.

Bert Keddie, Director General of the Victorian Department of Youth, Sport and Recreation, demonstrated by outstanding example that the words public service need not be an oxymoron. I could never find more dedicated and loyal colleagues than those invigorating days.

Thank you to Roy Lea who took a chance and offered me many challenging "insurmountable opportunities" at IBM. I also owe a great deal to the hundreds of colleagues I had the privilege to work with at IBM in Australia, Japan, and internationally.

A special thank you to Liz Burrows, for her section on Total Quality Management. And of course to Les Galbraith of American Express. I've been blessed to meet exceptional individuals like them in the course of my work and my life. It would be remiss of me if I did not also acknowledge all my clients and speaking bureaus that have provided opportunities to address thousands of people around the world. I've been able to listen to what those audiences have wanted to learn . . . and learned from sharing their own stories of service excellence.

Thank you to all those people who said: "You oughta write a book"; especially John Raedler and Michael Wrublewski for their unwavering encouragement to spread the service message in those early days, when no one wanted to listen.

Thank you to agent Robert Mackwood and the entire team at Career Press for believing that the customer service message is truly global.

And thanks to the Prentice Hall Australia and the Australian Institute of Management. Thanks to bookstores, and to you, the readers, who made the first edition a number one best seller. Without readers, an author is nothing.

Without friends, a person is nothing, so thanks to my friends for understanding I couldn't play golf or go to dinner while writing this. A much more renowned author, William Shakespeare, once said, "I am wealthy in my friends." He was surely a pauper compared with me in that regard! I would never dare compare this modest, but practical, book to the great literary volumes of Shakespeare, and I only hope it makes even a small contribution to better service to our customers and our planet.

INTRODUCTION

Turn common sense into common practice.

The Nobel prize is great, but for me the
best prize is to have readers.
—**Octavio Paz**
1990 Nobel literature prizewinner

Whether you're an employer or employee . . .
Whether you're in the private or public sector . . .
Whether you deal directly with customers
or work quietly behind the scenes . . .
Whether you like it or not . . .
YOU ALL HAVE CUSTOMERS!
Your employer does NOT pay your salary—
customers do!

Before exploring the latest management theories and practical examples of successful service organizations, let me first tell you a story, which may sound familiar . . .

Once upon a time, there was a little girl. Like most little girls, she grew into a teenager who wanted trendy clothes. That took money. She needed a job. Apart from babysitting and a paper run, her first "real" job was washing dishes at a golf club. She hated it. The boss was her father. She resented him telling her what to do. She dreaded his seemingly endless admonishments: "A job worth doing is worth doing well," and "Haste makes waste."

To make matters worse, when she wanted to spend her hard-earned money, her mother would add: "A penny saved is a penny earned," or "It's better to buy one good thing than five cheap things."

Those words fell on the deaf ears of a teenager. There were frequent disagreements around the dinner table when inevitably one parent would scold: "It's not what you say but the way you say it!""

Does this bring back childhood memories to you?

I was that young girl venturing into the world of work with the wrong attitude. If only I hadn't seen myself as a lousy dishwasher but recognized the important role I played in providing the customers with clean china and cutlery.

With their philosophies and principles, both my parents could have been management consultants today. I'm sure many readers can identify with their comments because they probably heard the same maxims from their own parents, which they treated with equal disdain. After all, what did Mom and Dad know? It's amazing how much smarter Dad became when I left my teens behind!

Even though my father died more than a quarter of a century ago, his teachings live on, as I often recall some of those pearls of wisdom, which are even more pertinent today than they were then. Thanks, Dad!

If you remember nothing else about the following chapters, please remember this:

> **The best customer relations is not to treat your customers like you treat your relations.**

Don't treat your customers as people you have to put up with; or take for granted . . . until it's too late!

Even the most sophisticated and most potent customer service strategies of today consist of nothing more than the common sense my parents tried to drum into me all those years ago . . . just as some management, likewise, tries to do to employees.

The aim of this book is to revisit some of those home truths, combined with research and case studies, to help turn common sense into common practice in your organization. By doing this, you will be able to gain the edge on your competitors and boost the bottom line.

As the title of this book states, "Good Service is Good Business" whether in the private or public sector. Better still, "Great Service is Great Business." Since this book was first published in 1994, and became a number-one best-seller in Australia, it's time for an international update that may already be out of date before the ink dries on the page, because customer service expectations are changing so rapidly with the growth of the Internet and services marketing.

Now, don't be disheartened; this provides an ideal opportunity for you to at least mentally add your own words to each chapter because no one understands the uniqueness of your workplace better than the people in it. And regardless of your position in the organization, you have a responsibility to focus on quality customer service, to make your own organization more competitive, and increase your nation's prospects of competing more advantageously globally.

This book was originally written for Australians by an Australian. But having since spoken to leading organizations on five continents, I know from unanimous client feedback that the principles contained within are truly global, with only minor cultural variations.

**Anyone who still thinks a customer isn't important . . .
should try doing without them for 90 days!**

Never did these words take on greater meaning than during a trip to Alaska where I'd spoken to a cruise conference. It was mid-May when we docked in Juneau, and brilliant sunshine reflected the snow-capped mountains in sparkling, clear blue waters. Disregarding the northern latitude, tourists enthusiastically disembarked from the ship in T-shirts.

We were greeted by the usual array of tour operators, never pushy and always friendly. But if tour operators weren't friendly, who would be? I thought. The whale-watching tour was magnificent, and we were treated to sightings of both killer and humpback whales on either side of the smaller boat we had boarded. Naturally, most visitors were in an exuberant mood to later wander around and shop. Without exception, I was impressed by the helpfulness and genuine warmth of the frontline staff in both the shops and restaurants.

In one shop, I waited while a customer verbally abused one of the staff over what seemed to me like a petty problem. I was impressed by how the salesperson handled the complaint and then cheerfully turned to me as if nothing had happened. I commented on her complaint-handling ability and said how wowed I was by everyone's approach to customer service where everyone seemed generally glad to have the place full of bargaining tourists.

"Of course we're glad to see you. You're the first customers we've had in six months!" she laughed. "The ice closes the waterway for much of the year." I asked if that meant I could expect everyone to have a totally different attitude and be grumpy at the end of the season. She laughed again and remarked: "You don't need to worry about that. Admittedly, we can get a little tired by then, but we know that when the last ship leaves for the season, it takes with it a precious cargo of customers."

Yes, in Alaska they fully comprehend that: "If you don't think a customer is important, just try doing without one for 90 days." (Or in their case, 180 days!)

This book contains highly acclaimed international quality service principles and strategies, as well as research data and some excerpts from a study done by AMR: Quantum. The study covered some 170 products and services, with a total response of 890 usable interviews. Their key findings, detailed more specifically in the book, show that compared with five years ago, Australians—like their overseas counterparts—are:

- More aware of customer service,
- Believe that the quality of customer service is about the same, but
- Have greater expectations of customer service, and, therefore
- Are less satisfied with customer service.

However, those suppliers of customer service believe that:

- Customers are more demanding, but
- They themselves are providing better customer service.

(AMR: Quantum, 1993)

There is no shortage of anecdotes outlining good and bad customer service. Many examples are outlined in the book.

Following the many presentations I've given to large and small businesses and government departments, I often receive requests for recommended books to read on the subject of quality service and pleas for suggestions on improving customer service. This book does not contain any earth-shattering academic revelations or magical formulas for overnight windfalls. It would be wonderful to find a hidden secret of successful service. It would make a great title for a book and I was tempted to call this "Seven Secrets of Service Success." But the fact remains that there are no easy secrets to success in service or any other endeavor.

The only time success comes before work is in the dictionary.

There are no mysteries to the long-term, worldwide success of a McDonald's or a Disney. Hamburger recipes and clean washrooms are not supervised by CIA agents in trench coats.

I repeat, there are no secrets to service success!

But there are many strategies that, through consistent implementation, have resulted in successful organizations. This book has divided these strategies into an easy-to-identify service mnemonic/model:

S   Self-esteem
E   Exceed expectations
R   Recover
V   Vision
I   Improve
C   Care
E   Empowerment

This book does not provide a panacea for service problems. It identifies the state-of-the-art management thinking and illustrates such academic wisdom with practical examples.

I encourage readers to view the research and analogies in light of what may or may not work in their own organization. Some of the many illustrations provided will definitely assist in improving your customer service levels.

We've been conditioned to keep books in pristine, mint condition. Don't! Get a pen (or pencil if you are reluctant) and make notes in the margin or use a highlighter as you read about the various aspects of service in successful companies. Not all will be relevant to your organization, but many will inevitably trigger your own ideas that can be readily implemented.

Service is often the first thing that is mentioned and the last thing that is done. There is no better time to start than now. If business is booming, you can increase your competitive edge. And even in tough economic times, quality service is free. A smile, eye contact, and cheerful voice cost nothing but do boost the bottom line. Reducing errors saves the cost of rework and results in increased profitability.

Few businesses make a deliberate decision to offer poor or mediocre service, but the successful ones actively focus on continuous improvement. They don't fall into the trap of saying they didn't have time to do the job right but do have the time to do it over again! Wherever they may be geographically based in the world, they change the old Australian saying, "She'll be right mate," [it will turn out okay] to "Get it right mate." Like good mates and friends, they recognize the value of true partnerships with customers. They comprehend that courtesy means business. And that business means jobs.

**Courtesy is like air in your tires. It doesn't cost
anything but makes travel more pleasant.**
—Miguel Cruzatta

1 Self-esteem

- **EXCEED EXPECTATIONS**

- **RECOVER**

- **VISION**

- **IMPROVE**

- **CARE**

- **EMPOWERMENT**

*Happy employees
yield happier customers*

If a man is called to be a street sweeper,
he should sweep streets
even as Michelangelo painted
or Beethoven composed music
or Shakespeare wrote poetry.
He should sweep streets so well
that all the hosts of heaven and earth
will pause to say, here lived
a great street sweeper who did his job well.
—Martin Luther King

1   Service is not subservience

Service comes from people . . . not companies. Without self-esteem, we have nothing. It's no different in organizations, which essentially are only collections of individuals.

High self-esteem is an essential ingredient for any successful service organization. If employees feel good about themselves and who they work for, some of that positive outlook transfers to the customer.

In the Western world, we have too often confused service with subservience and sometimes felt it was beneath our dignity to "serve" another.

Dictionaries offer many definitions of the word service. Two examples are:

1. "The attendance of an inferior upon a superior,"
   or
2. "To be useful."

It's imperative to alter our attitude to implant the last definition firmly as the norm. Service does not have to be subservient. Serving is not something you do before you get a "real" job or the sole prerogative of third-world countries. "To be useful" is a goal that everyone can easily identify with and aspire toward.

In September 1997, I heard the Dalai Lama speak to 10,000 people. When asked a question about the meaning of life, something we all ask ourselves from time to time, he smiled and simply responded:

There are two meanings of life—to be happy and to be useful.

Although I'm not sure that this answer adequately answered my own questions about the meaning of life, his comment certainly aroused my curiosity and, upon further investigation, I learned that such thoughts are not restricted to Buddhist beliefs. In fact, in the Bible, Jesus is quoted as saying: "Those who wish to be great amongst you should also serve." Hindu, Muslim, and Jewish friends inform me that there are similar teachings in their faiths and a former IBM colleague now studying theology assured me that the concept of being useful was an underlying theme in virtually every religion in the world.

I'm not advocating any particular religious base, but rather a general philosophy of being useful as individuals while we are on this planet. And since so much of our time is spent at work, it seems only sensible that employees approach their everyday tasks with the fundamental premise that they are in fact being useful to those they serve. This would result in a tremendous shift in customer satisfaction levels, rather than the all too frequent attitude of "I just work here." And if all workers adopted that attitude, they would likewise be happier as well during their working hours. Even if they were employed at a job that they didn't see as their lifetime career, they could better enjoy their time on that task.

An estimated 70 percent of employment will be in the services sector in the years following the millennium. If we ignore the value of service quality, it is at our peril.

In a more deregulated and increasingly competitive marketplace, industry is discovering just how important service is. To be internationally competitive in terms of gross domestic product (GDP) per capita, we all need to focus on continuous improvement. Like highly skilled athletes, service champions need to give their "personal best" to give customers what they want . . . when they want it.

It is a goal that, if achieved, will improve our individual standards of living by making a significant contribution to the overall economy.

In fact, it is one every nation must achieve to remain globally competitive. A tongue-in-cheek comment I once saw states:

> *Seen boarding a China Airlines Labor Transporter aircraft at Los Angeles airport, this group of young Americans are reported to have secured five-year contracts as laundry maids in Taipei. "This is a fantastic opportunity," gushed Mandy Baker. "A friend of mine was able to move up to a Grade 2 bar girl and is now engaged to a Vladivostok chartered accountant."*

Although an obvious exaggeration, the above comment serves to remind us of the importance to focus on how globalization and invisible borders, created by e-commerce, have changed service levels forever...in some instances for better, in others, for worse.

2 Excellence starts at the top— leadership by example

The Ritz Carlton's credo of "Ladies and gentlemen serving ladies and gentlemen" quickly dispels the notion that service is beneath anyone's dignity.

It and the Hyatt Hotel chains are consistently rated tops in the world. In those hotels, everyone is conditioned to be thoroughly committed to serving the customer. For example, the president of Hyatt International occasionally sheds his expensive business suit to don a bellhop's uniform and carry bags for the guests. This brings him closer to his customers, who are not likely to feel inhibited telling a bellboy what they really think about the hotel. More important, this role reversal has the advantage of conveying a message to all employees that service at the Hyatt isn't beneath the dignity of anyone!

Service leadership starts at the top and service leaders practice what they preach. They set the standards for everyone in the organization. Thomas Watson, Sr., founder of IBM, would eat in the employees' cafeteria and make a point of quietly stooping down to pick up any stray napkins. Likewise, Ray Croc, founder of McDonald's, would often wander into a franchise with a piece of garbage he had removed from the parking lot and ask the store manager why he couldn't do so, himself. This corporate culture lives on. Chris Simpson, owner/operator of McDonald's at Coffs Harbour on the eastern shores of Australia, was holding a breakfast business meeting at his franchise when we noticed a dog foul the parking lot. Much to our surprise, Chris politely excused himself and immediately went out with a shovel to personally dispose of the mess. He could easily have asked a junior employee to do the dirty work, but his personal actions were more powerful in conveying a message to all staff about standards of cleanliness.

Disney management must spend two weeks every year as frontline staff to gain a better appreciation of what really happens in their fun parks. The street sweeper, ice-cream vendor, ride attendant, or person behind the Mickey Mouse mask may well be a highly paid executive.

Surely, this doesn't imply that the president of a bank should spend some time as a teller? Or, the CEO of the Postal Service sort mail? Or, the managing director of a supermarket chain work at a checkout? Or, the head of the education department help in a school?

Yes!

Naturally, this would only be a very small portion of their roles, but occasional hands-on experience at the front line would be invaluable to them and the thousands of employees under their leadership.

Certainly, there are limits. I'd be delighted if I saw the president of United Airlines checking in baggage, but horrified if he tried to fly the plane!

Each year, all IBM managers, whether in sales or not, are asked to make customer calls. Executives of a funds management company in Western Australia are required to call five customers per day just to say hello and ask if everything is satisfactory. And, the CEO of their affiliate bank has been seen in an apron, serving pancakes to branch customers at a "thank-you breakfast." I know there are many other examples of executives occasionally venturing forth from the corner office to roll up their sleeves and get closer to the customer and frontline staff. Naturally, in an industrial climate, demarcation issues must be considered to determine the appropriateness of such actions.

Hands-on leadership need not be the exclusive domain of private enterprise. The principal of a primary school in Melbourne, Jan Shrimpton, visits each grade every day. Jan has made a tremendous transformation in that school by focusing on customer service and treating teachers and pupils with respect and not recrimination.

Respect for the individual is the underlying principle of IBM's highly acclaimed management practices. It isn't some lukewarm personnel slogan but a belief articulated by the founder, and the foundation of everything the organization does to motivate employees. Ms. Shrimpton never had the opportunity to attend IBM management classes but could certainly teach managers a thing or two about staff relations and self-esteem. At the start of each staff meeting, teachers are encouraged to share a positive experience. She reinforces each one with a specific comment relevant to what she has observed: "What I like about your teaching is. . . ."

Respect for the staff transfers to respect for the pupils. Every child is well aware of the consequences of unacceptable behavior, but is encouraged with positive reinforcement. Teachers on playground duty are given raffle tickets to reward pupils who behave well. These need not be the school "goody-goodies," but those who play quietly, respect others, or dispose of litter. Each day, one ticket is drawn and the holder is given the opportunity to choose a granola bar or fluorescent-colored marking pen. At the end of each month, pupils with the most raffle tickets visit the local McDonald's with the principal. Staff morale is up and delinquencies among pupils are down.

3   Treat employees as you want them to treat customers

A maxim of modern management is to treat employees the way you would want them to treat customers...and make them feel good about themselves and your organization.

A bank employee in Launceston, Tasmania dreaded lunch hour when she walked down the street in uniform. She was sometimes harassed by bank customers who angrily suggested she should be in the bank serving so the lines wouldn't be so long. The fact that she wasn't a teller made no difference to their perception; and certainly it did nothing to mend her own damaged self-image. Launceston or Los Angeles—the same holds true!

Often, the perceptions of individual employees are vastly different from the realities. A designer-fashioned corporate uniform did nothing for this young woman's self-esteem. Yet, in many cases, the sense of belonging created by such a uniform can make a huge difference. Servicemen from the gas company in Japan arrive at your door in blue suits and convey not only an air of efficiency, but look, for all intents and purposes, like executives. And they act like executives.

Titles can also make a difference to employees' perceptions of their roles. The term *shop assistant* is meaningless. It implies that the person is assisting the shop, rather than the customer within it. Why not call the same person a *customer consultant*? The job would be the same, but the employee's self-image wouldn't be. Naturally, such superficial changes do not make a service success but are small fine-tunings that may add to self-esteem.

At Disneyland the street sweepers, ice-cream servers, and ride attendants are referred to as "The Cast," and whenever they're in front of a customer, they are "on stage." McDonald's frontline staff is known as "Crew." Such symbolism, if linked with other substantial service strategies, can contribute to overall success.

Nordstrom, one of the most successful retailers in the United States, uses more than symbolism to treat their staff with respect. The average sales staff member in the United States, near the end of the last century, earned $15,000 to 19,000 per year. At Nordstrom, they earned $70,000 to 80,000 per year, as a result of commissions on sales (Zemke and Schaaf, 1989). Management empowers all employees to do the right thing by the customer. Some industry experts claim that Nordstrom overstocks and overstaffs, but Nordstrom is still one of the most profitable retailers in the United States. How can this be? Their success is attributed to legendary service.

An executive of one of Nordstrom competitors found this hard to believe, so he decided to shop at Nordstrom. He bought two suits and became smug when they couldn't be delivered before he went on an interstate trip. When he checked into his hotel room, the two suits had been sent by courier, with two free silk ties. No sales representative needed to obtain authorization from a supervisor to do this (Blanchard). Dr. Ken Blanchard told this anecdote in an excellent video, *Legendary Service*. Blanchard also gave another example of wishing to use a telephone at a competitor's department store. The salesperson said it was impossible because: "Management won't even allow me to use the phone so we certainly couldn't let customers use it!" As a customer, Blanchard made the same request at Nordstrom and was able to use the phone. A lot of good service can relate to the trust and respect that the company shows the employee that, in turn, results in higher self-esteem.

What a contrast to visiting a major retailer in Sydney. I discovered I had lost my credit card and asked the cashier if I could use the phone to cancel the card and pay cash for the purchase. She informed me there was a rule that customers weren't allowed to use the phone for personal calls. I said I could appreciate the rule, but this was not a chatty call and that, if I used my credit card, she would have made a phone call, anyway, to validate my account.

She agreed with me but had to check with the supervisor. I could see the supervisor abruptly say no and admonish her for even thinking of "breaking a rule." I left the store without the two pairs of shoes and have never been back to that particular store since.

Shortly after, I had the opportunity to shop at Nordstrom in San Francisco. I had read about their excellent service, but believed the tales must have certainly been an exaggeration. I walked into the shoe department and was immediately asked if I wanted help. I said I was interested in a pair of gray suede shoes. I was shown to a seat and within a short time, a saleswoman arrived with two pairs. She also produced a brand new stocking so that I might try on the shoes hygienically. During our brief interlude, she chatted pleasantly and asked how I was enjoying San Francisco. I decided to buy one pair of shoes even though the left shoe seemed a bit tighter than the right. On closer inspection, one shoe was an 81/2A and the other an 81/2B. For some reason, there had been a mix-up in the shoebox and I asked if it was possible to have a pair that were both 81/2B. The sales clerk expressed concern and returned immediately to say that she was terribly sorry but there had been a mix-up before and another customer had obviously received the other mismatched pair.

In reality, a customer may well have made the change, but the saleswoman made no such implication. She was only concerned with the customer at hand and offered me a discount if I bought the mismatched pair. As there wasn't a great difference in the two shoes, I did so.

She then surprised me further by asking, "If you have time to wait another minute, I'd like to offer you a free protective treatment to prevent any water damage."

By now, I already believed the service at Nordstrom was exceptional. But, it got even better. She noticed I had a number of miscellaneous parcels from other shops and asked if I would like to consolidate them all into a big bag (with a Nordstrom name, of course). Then she offered a free shuttle service from the store back to my hotel...all without checking with a supervisor! Needless to say, I was impressed and asked what sort of training she had received to give such great service. She said that she had to be fully conversant with the merchandise and added: "At Nordstrom, there are only two rules of customer service:

Rule Number One: Use your own good judgment at all times.
Rule Number Two: There are no other rules!"

By the way, I didn't take advantage of the free shuttle, but went to the clothing department where I was greeted by a woman who said: "Hello, I'm Joan. It's nice to meet you," and offered me her outstretched hand to shake. After I picked myself up from shock, I recovered to buy two suits, which I hadn't intended to. But the staff had turned an otherwise mundane shopping task into a pleasant experience.

A couple of years later, I visited a different Nordstrom, also in California, but I'd have thought I was on a different planet, rather than simply in a different store. After an initial greeting, I was completely ignored and left stranded in the fitting room for 15 minutes, with a promise of someone to help with alterations. When I eventually gave up and went to the counter to purchase one item, instead of potentially three, the salesperson suddenly appeared, as they receive commission on their sales. I informed her how disappointed I was and that I was purchasing the one garment in spite of her service, rather than because of it! I indicated that she'd let down the good name of Nordstrom, when she blurted out in defense: "It's not my fault. We're understaffed today because everyone is at a customer service course!"

Who was at fault—the salesperson, the management, or both? And what's the moral of the story?

Service in any organization, regardless of reputation, is only as good as you get at any one point in time from any one individual!

Service providers should eliminate no from the vocabulary of employees. Rather than look at problems, look at ways to say yes and help a customer in any given situation. For example, if a customer wishes to withdraw funds from a fixed term deposit, the teller could respond in one of two ways:

- "No, you can't do that without losing interest."
- "Yes, you certainly can do that if you wish, but I need to advise you that there will be some loss of interest."

The second option then gives the customer a choice and is a much more positive approach to the same situation.

4 Take time to hire positive people in the first place

Hire positive people and dismiss those who harbor negative attitudes. There is an old saying that: "It is easier to change people than it is to change people." In other words, as difficult as it may be to dismiss someone with a negative attitude, there is only so much counseling management can do to alter that approach.

Smart managers invest the time to hire the right person in the first place. It takes time to devise an appropriate advertisement, outlining your expectations of serving customers. It takes time to sort through applications. And, it certainly takes time to interview applicants. But, it's better to invest this time to obtain the best person than settle for someone you're not sure about. If management adopts a "near enough is good enough" approach to hiring, those employees will adopt that same attitude toward customers. If you're not sure that the person will fit in and have the same high standards that you do . . . don't hire him or her, even if it means the hassle and expense of re-advertising.

Hire people with high energy, enthusiasm, and a positive outlook. Naturally, you also want to obtain people with as much experience and skill as possible, but you can teach people skills to gain experience. It is much harder to alter attitudes.

A well-known Brisbane hotel hires on three factors—personality, personality, and personality! It's a bit like real estate where the buyer is asked to look for location, location, and location.

Following the initial interviews for management trainees at McDonald's in Australia, part of the selection process is to spend a couple of days in the franchise to determine whether the applicant likes the environment. This also allows management to assess whether the applicants have the right attitude for the job.

McDonald's, like other leading service organizations, looks for people who feel good about themselves. How can you determine this at an interview? Ask potential employees questions such as:

- How do you enjoy dealing with customers?
- What do you like most about your current position?
- What do you like least about your current position?
- Can you give me an example of how you have delighted a customer?
- What steps did you take in an instance when someone was unhappy?

Then give them a real-life customer service situation, which actually happened in your organization, and ask how they would respond to it. Better still, you play the irate customer and have them role-play their response.

To people looking for work, you can never be too positive, as long as you are also sincere in your answers.

5   Take an interest in your job to make it more interesting

If you take an interest in your job, does it become more interesting?

The role of a toll-collector on a turnpike wouldn't generally be regarded as the most exciting job in the world. The story, one I'm sorry

I can't quote the source of, as I heard it at a conference many years ago, is told of one such toll-collector on the Golden Gate Bridge in San Francisco. The traffic authorities couldn't explain why there was always a long line of traffic at this one particular gate. Upon closer inspection, they discovered a young man who had pop music blaring away as he danced in his booth and greeted early morning commuters with a cheery word and smile. It didn't take any more time than the other lanes but motorists intentionally changed lanes to get a good start to their day.

After interviewing motorists to determine that there was no dissatisfaction (in fact, the responses were quite the opposite), the traffic authorities approached this young man to ask why he seemed to be having such a good time in what they saw as a mundane job. His response staggered them. It was along the lines of:

> *Hey man, me and my music are having a party here with all these nice people. One day, I want to be a dancer but in the meantime, I can practice my rhythm and make people happy while I collect their money. Look at these other toll-takers. It looks more like they're in vertical coffins than tollbooths. Happy? Yeah...why shouldn't I be happy? I've got a corner office with glass on all sides and great views that many executives would kill for. Of course, I'm happy in my job. What's the point of being miserable?*

It's all in how you see your job.

The same lesson can be learned from the story of two bricklayers working on St. Paul's Cathedral. One man was approached and asked what he was doing. "Can't you see I'm laying bricks, you fool?" was the reply.

The other bricklayer responded: "I'm helping Sir Christopher Wren build a glorious cathedral."

The earlier question is answered: *Yes, if you take an interest in your job, it does become more interesting*!

There are no interesting jobs. Only jobs...the interest is built in by you, the individual!

A business acquaintance recently did some training at Sydney's Regent Hotel and told me of the dishwasher who remarked: "I'm the backbone of this hotel."

And so he is! All employees need to have that attitude and positive self-esteem, and management needs to ensure that every employee, regardless of his or her status in the organizational hierarchy, is made to feel his or her role is very important.

Filing clerks aren't really paid to file documents. Their own self-esteem could be greatly enhanced if they realized they play a critical role in the organization because of their ability to be able to readily *retrieve* the information in those documents.

You may not be able to train people to have a positive attitude, but training can still play a vital role in raising the self-esteem of employees. If they have the proper skills and believe the company is interested in investing in their development to make them better employees, there will be a spin-off to the way in which they treat customers.

Service quality training will be covered more extensively in Chapter 5, but it is worth a brief mention here in regard to self-esteem. At Disneyland, the street sweepers are the highest paid casual employees, and receive 4–10 days' training, even 12-week holiday students. Disney discovered that visitors were more likely to ask street sweepers for information than the formal customer-relations staff. And Disney believes that training is important for everyone—not just up-and-coming executives.

In service-focused organizations, training is continuous. It needs to be because service is an intangible product. Unlike other products, it has no shelf life and is only as good as what is delivered at any time. The $10 notes you receive from any bank are exactly the same product. It is the service that differentiates one bank from another.

6   Success today doesn't guarantee success tomorrow

More than ever before, we need to ensure people in service jobs are regarded, and regard themselves, highly. We need to dispel any notion that a service occupation is a temporary measure.

We must recognize the change in the service environment. We need to realize that customers have higher expectations than ever before. That may seem like bad news, but it's really good news because if you rise to the challenge, a career in the service industry can be both personally and financially rewarding.

In business we need to pay close attention to changes in the environment. We need to stop...to reassess the service cultures of our organizations and ask if what we did to be successful yesterday will be appropriate for continued success in the future. No matter how successful an organization is today, no leader can assume that what worked well yesterday will be successful tomorrow.

Jan Carlzon, once the chief executive officer of Scandinavian Airlines, turned the business from an $18 million loss to a $54 million profit. He says this about the change in outlook of his organization that led to success:

> *In the 1980s, we saw a customer in every individual.*
> *In the 1990s, we see an individual in every customer.*
> —(Carlzon, 1987)

It may seem to be a subtle change, but it was an immense difference in the way employees were asked to view each and every customer situation then. It applies even more so in this new millennium. Every employee in the organization was given responsibility for improving customer service. It wasn't beneath anyone's dignity to serve, and Carlzon, himself, took an active role to deliver service and ensure high self-esteem among staff.

S E V E N   K E Y   P O I N T S
in this chapter on self-esteem:

1 Service is not subservience.

2 Service excellence starts at the top—leadership by example.

3 Treat employees as you want them to treat customers.

4 Take time to hire positive staff in the first place.

5 Take an interest in your job to make it more interesting.

6 Success today does not guarantee success tomorrow.

7 In my own organization, I will improve service through self-esteem by:

_____

_____

_____

_____

_____

_____

_____

_____

■ SELF—ESTEEM

2 Exceed Expectations

■ RECOVER

■ VISION

■ IMPROVE

■ CARE

■ EMPOWERMENT

Promise good. Deliver great!
—Motto of *T.G.I. Friday's*

1 Set, meet, and exceed expectations to stand out in the market

Many organizations make the mistake of creating unreasonably high customer expectations. Where they fail is in providing no more than mediocre products or services. Unfulfilled promises may get customers through the door or ordering off the World Wide Web the first time, but will not result in repeat business.

The most elaborate advertising campaigns are useless if they create an unrealistic customer expectation and the organization is then unable to provide the promised level of service. Clever organizations set high standards of customer service and clearly communicate those standards to customers and staff. They don't promise what they can't deliver, and they work hard to meet expectations that they have created among customers. What's more, they work even harder to exceed those expectations and turn simply satisfied customers into delighted ones.

Exceeding customer expectations does not necessarily cost more money. It can have quite the opposite effect.

You walk into a five-star hotel and are greeted by a student in a baseball cap who asks: "Would you like a milk shake with your burger?" This would hardly meet, let alone exceed, your expectations of a five-star hotel.

You arrive at a McDonald's and are greeted by an elegantly dressed maître d' who escorts you to your table. The table is covered with lovely linen, silver, fine china, crystal, flowers, and candles. A violinist plays softly in the background. Would this exceed your expectations of McDonald's?

Yes.

But as you munch away on your Big Mac, you realize this must certainly cost more money and take more time. And the service expectation that McDonald's has set for consumers worldwide is cheap fast food. By providing all those extras, McDonald's would not really be exceeding the customer expectations that they have so carefully set. All the extra trimmings would not be considered to add value to your McDonald's experience.

It is important to know exactly what the customer expects of service standards within your own organization. More important, you need to help set customer expectation levels so you do not waste time, effort, and dollars on what customers may regard as unnecessary.

One of my early jobs was as a cook on an oil rig in the middle of nowhere in northern Canada. Because of the isolation, most of the food was frozen and canned. As a special treat to the roughnecks, and with considerable effort on my part, I thought I would create delighted customers by providing them with a fresh fruit salad instead of the normal canned product. I had fresh fruit flown in, and I chopped and peeled for much longer than it would have taken to open a can. I didn't mind as I thought their appreciation would be worth the effort. Much to my surprise, the general reaction was not one of gratitude, but rather resulted in comments such as:

"Have you run out of canned fruit?"

Not to be deterred, I went to the trouble of making bread one day. A few were most grateful but again, the majority inquired after the packaged loaves. I hadn't taken into consideration that many of these men had not been accustomed to fresh food for years. Their taste buds were conditioned to processed food, and when I thought I was exceeding their expectations, I was only wasting my efforts. I hadn't taken the trouble to find out what my customers really expected. Had I understood anything about customer service, I could have easily exceeded their expectations by providing a larger helping of canned fruit or packaged bread. It would have been more cost- and time-effective for me, and they would have been happier.

Customer expectations are very specific in terms of industry, market position, geographic location, and so on. For example, when visiting Buenos Aires, I was told that when Pizza Hut first opened in Argentina, like Pizza Huts worldwide, they had paper place mats on the tables. Business was slow. The situation improved dramatically when paper place mats were replaced with linen tablecloths because, apparently, that was a minimum expectation of dining standards in Argentina at the time.

In this instance, unlike the previous McDonald's example, the tablecloth was perceived in the eyes of the customer as adding value to the fast food experience. We all need to consider what the equivalent of a "tablecloth" is in our own business and make sure that we spend our limited time and resources on those furnishings and activities that are truly adding value to the customer—not simply cost to our bottom line.

You'll notice that most hotels have a sign in the bathroom encouraging you to reuse the towels to save precious water to protect the environment. Interestingly enough, this notion first started in Tasmania when conservation became a major issue during the 1980s and eco-tourism was in its embryonic days. Guests in that environment would be more likely to accept that notion, rather than automatically expect towels to be washed every night, as we seldom do at home. One can't help but be a little cynical that most hotels today do so for cost-saving reasons rather than environmental concerns. But it's still a good thing as, in most instances, clean towels every day don't add significant value to your stay (although I still know a couple of people who see it as a luxury they wouldn't have at home). What's more, there are now signs on bed linen suggesting that you may not want your sheets freshly laundered every night during your stay.

Likewise, with the growth in the number of small shareholders, companies saw their printing and postage costs escalate with the increased production of annual reports. Many astute investors studied the share trading and financial details and looked at all the glossy pictures but many more, like me, probably just threw that expensive publication in the garbage. That's why it came as no surprise when I started to notice that most companies now ask shareholders to nominate whether or not we'd like to receive the annual report. However, no company has been willing to share with me the extent of cost savings by implementing this measure, which to many shareholders would only be adding cost to the bottom line.

A few years ago, long before the introduction of electronic airline ticketing, I challenged one of my clients, a leader in the travel industry, to look at their equivalent of the hypothetical "tablecloth" at McDonald's. As a frequent business traveler, I pointed out that the little plastic folders that business travelers received every trip were only adding cost, not value.

"Oh no, people expect them, we couldn't possibly get rid of them," was the initial reaction. And, although they didn't initially eliminate plastic folders completely, they did start asking frequent travelers if they would like them and, subsequently, the costs associated with obtaining the plastic ticket folders reduced dramatically.

Again ask the question:

What is the equivalent of the tablecloth or plastic folder in my organization?

There are no set rules and businesses must consider the expectations of their own clients. They must then proceed to reinforce those expectations and strive to exceed them.

T.G.I. Friday's is a very successful restaurant chain, started in the United States and now in other parts of the world. All their staff members are well aware of the company motto: "Promise Good and Deliver Great." They promise customers high-quality food in a pleasant environment. They aim to deliver quality food in a fun-filled environment and even suggest alterations to the combinations printed on the menu.

Another restaurant in Sydney offers not only main course and entree sizes but gives customers the additional option of a one-and-a-half entree size!

It is important to know what the market expects. Expectation, price, and delivery need to be aligned. Five-star service in a five-star hotel—but do not expect it in a youth hostel.

Assuming you have a sound product that is appropriately priced, expectations will differentiate your organization in the marketplace, according to Professor Levitt of the Harvard Business School (Levitt 1980). Professor Levitt provides a three-ringed model, which, even though developed in 1980, stands the test of time (see Figure 2.1).

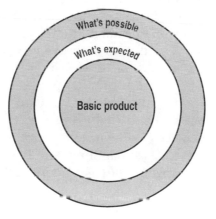

FIGURE 2.1   Three-ringed expectation model.

Adapted from Theodore Levitt, "Marketing Success Through Differentiation—of Anything:; in *Harvard Business Review,* Jan/Feb 1980, p. 86.

- At the core of the circle is the basic product. For example, in the airline industry, the basic product is safe transport between destinations.
- The next ring is what is expected or meeting customer expectations. For example, in the airline industry, the simple expectation is a reasonably comfortable seat, clean toilet, and refreshments.
- The outer ring is what is possible or exceeding customer expectations to create delighted customers. It is this outer ring that can prove the differentiating factor between successful and unsuccessful organizations. For example, in the airline industry, an economy customer would have expectations exceeded by having their favorite magazine, video game, champagne, and a charming flight attendant.

It is critical that all three circles of this market differentiation model be aligned. For example, in the airline industry, it would be pointless for a passenger to be sipping the finest French champagne, and the attendant saying "Have a nice day" if the wing were falling off the basic product!

Qantas, Australia's national carrier, is well regarded by Australians and visitors alike and a large part of that choice must relate to its safety record. Qantas also works hard to provide excellent service and, although passenger surveys of the best service vary from time to time, Qantas is always among the leaders. So too is Ansett, the other main airline in Australia, but it won't be long until they face increased competition from the likes of Virgin, who is always striving to exceed passenger expectations.

Flying hundreds of thousands of miles per year to speak at conferences around the world, I must say that standards, even within the same airline, vary from flight to flight and it's consistency that is crucial. Certainly, my choice is influenced by price, schedules, timeliness, seat comfort, food, baggage handling, and how I'm treated as a member of their loyalty program. But as a frequent flier, it's the little things that make me feel good; make me feel a little special when I'm weary and away from home.

For example, I did a coast-to-coast tour where I spoke at a breakfast meeting in a different city every day for two weeks. The client and

I traveled together and, naturally, we were tired near the end of the tour. On the second to last flight, neither of us ate the main course, which consisted of rather fatty chicken, and settled for the bread and salad. When the flight attendant asked why we hadn't eaten the chicken, we commented that it was a bit fatty and we were conscious of healthy eating.

With personality plus, the young airline employee agreed and humorously pointed out that we'd eaten the butter with our bread, which was also high in cholesterol. We all had a bit of a laugh, discussing the pros and cons of different sorts of fat in diets, as we arrived on the last flight into town that evening.

The next day, with only one flight left on this somewhat tiring tour, we happened to have the same flight attendant who, as we boarded the plane, burst into a big smile and said jovially: "Oh hello—here are the two fat ladies again!"

Now, this would not normally be a greeting one would view favorably, but since neither of us was overweight and we knew it was said in good humor, we burst out laughing. The attendant had remembered us and not simply reverted to the standard "Have a nice day" but treated us as he would have a good friend, even though I was old enough to be his mother.

Both my client and I remembered that as the highlight of our two weeks in the air. We both commented we'd be choosing that airline to fly on for the foreseeable future (unless someone else did something to make us change back to another!).

A few weeks later I was rushing through another airport for a flight with the same airline. Being a little nearsighted, I had trouble reading the monitor, so breathlessly asked the young attendant: "Is this Melbourne?" "No, not yet," he replied, touching me gently on the arm, steering me in the direction of the gate. "But it will be in one hour so may I suggest you just relax and enjoy the flight."

Now, I appreciate that calling women fat or physically touching them could be a "dangerous" thing to do, and I suppose I'd have to generally caution service providers against doing such things as there could always be a minority who wouldn't appreciate the heartfelt gestures or could misinterpret them. However, someone truly excellent at service instinctively knows when it's okay to break the rules and exceed customer expectations of "one size fits all" treatment.

It's also important to first set customer expectations. If you paid to see a Rolling Stones concert and were greeted by the Berlin Symphony Orchestra, you would be disappointed; and vice versa. Both would draw sell-out crowds and are excellent entertainment . . . but different!

As products improve, so do customer expectations. Not that long ago new car buyers were concerned with whether the car would operate or not. As the reliability of the product has increased, so have customer expectations. Now the key concerns of new car buyers are wind noise and drink holders.

Disneyland provides an excellent example of having a good product and then meeting and exceeding customer expectations. Most visitors to Disneyland, when asked of their first impressions, seldom rave about Space Mountain, Frontierland, or Mickey Mouse. Comments generally relate to the cleanliness and friendliness of the environment. The amusements (products) are taken for granted by the customer. This does not mean that Disney does not focus on maintaining that basic product. If there were any safety problems with these amusements then that would become an area of customer focus. Disney makes sure every employee appreciates the role they play in providing a safe product and meeting customer expectations.

They set realistic customer expectations in every regard. Many of their popular rides have long lines. Since management can't control daily demand, they post signs outside every line, estimating the length of the wait. They then provide entertainment for families standing in the line, to make the time pass more pleasantly.

In terms of exceeding customer expectations, Disney is equally clever. If a ride is advertised as having a 45-minute wait, a customer makes a choice to stand in that line and has an expectation of the required wait. Inevitably, the 45-minute waits are more like 40, and the 20-minute waits are 15. Disney is setting customer expectations and then exceeding them. It's much more palatable to be told there is a 30-minute wait and then wait only 20 than to be told there's a 20-minute wait and wait 30. Disney underpromises and overdelivers. This reduces anxiety of both the client and management.

A car dealer in Sydney uses this principle equally effectively. He learned that drivers become agitated when car repairs take longer than anticipated. However, he also discovered that they don't mind nearly as much if they are given a better car to drive while theirs is in for repair. Another dealer provides cell phones to customers who don't have their own so he can contact them the moment the car is ready.

2 Service boosts your bottom line

The challenge any business faces is how to close the service gap between what customers expect and what they perceive is delivered.

The Profit Impact of Marketing Strategy (PIMS) survey conducted in the United States provides powerful evidence that customer perceptions of service can actually make a difference to the bottom-line financial results. The research surveyed customer databases of 3,000 suppliers of goods and services. Companies were classified by their customers as "service leaders" or "poor providers." These customer perceptions were then matched with how the organizations actually performed in the marketplace.

Traditional marketing management believed that the only strategies were to cut price, add more services, run more specials, increase advertising, and look for technological breakthroughs. Service, as a competitive edge, was considered "soft" stuff. The PIMS research showed none of the traditional strategies gave an organization a sustained competitive advantage but the "soft" service stuff did. Let's look at some "hard" research data:

- The perceived service leaders could charge 9-10 percent more for the same basic good or service.
- The perceived service leaders grew twice as fast as their competition.
- The perceived service leaders improved their market share up to 6 percent per year.
- The perceived poor service providers lost as much as 2 percent market share per year.
- The perceived service leaders had a return on sales 12 percent higher than the perceived poor providers.

(Zemke and Schaaf 1989)

It is important to note there was no data to verify whether the companies were in fact providing good or bad service. The data related solely to customer perceptions. Whether customer perceptions are right or wrong, it is almost impossible to argue with them, as they soon become reality in the minds of the customer.

3 You can't argue with customer perception

An example of this is provided by Stu Leonard's supermarket in Stanford, Conn.

As a customer-focused organization, the manager would hold regular breakfast meetings with customers to elicit their opinions on the store. At one of these meetings, a woman mentioned the fish was quite good but would be even better if it were fresh. He asked what she meant by this comment as the fish was, in fact, obtained fresh every morning. She argued that it couldn't possibly be fresh because it was packaged in Styrofoam and plastic wrap.

Rather than try to convince her that she had an incorrect perception of the product, the store decided on a test—as a result of this one customer complaint. When the fresh fish arrived the next day, half was packaged as previously and the other half was laid out on crushed ice. Much to management's amazement, the same fish laid on the ice resulted in double the sales in the first week alone!

Stu Leonard's customers are greeted by a huge rock at the entrance, which reads:

There are two rules of customer service . . .
1. The customer is always right!
2. If the customer is wrong, reread rule number 1!

By following this creed and listening to one customer complaint about the fish (which was in fact a totally incorrect perception) the store became the winner.

The store's financial performance is indeed an impressive one as a result of its focus on quality service. The average industry sales in a shop equivalent of Stu Leonard's are $300 per square foot per day. His turnover was a staggering $3,000 per square foot per day! Listening to the customer pays!

But, so does honesty! And although I've been informed that it would appear that Stu Leonard had some unfortunate issues with the Internal Revenue Service, this in no way diminishes the relevance of this specific story.

A Rothmans Australia employee, Rod McLaughlin, once gave me an excellent example of an inaccurate customer perception. They had apparently received numerous complaints from a woman about the flavor of their cigarettes. Whenever they receive a complaint, Rothmans provides the customer with a carton of cigarettes as compensation. Their records showed this woman continually complained about a musk flavor in the tobacco and received numerous cartons of cigarettes.

They suspected that she might have fabricated the complaints as a means to obtain free cigarettes. They called her in to meet with management and tour the production facility. In the process, they discovered her complaint was, in fact, genuine, but the blame lay with her. She often carried her cigarettes in a small handbag that also usually contained musk-flavored Lifesavers. As tobacco is a porous substance, the taste was easily absorbed.

The end result was a happy customer who had complained in all honesty and Rothmans was no longer concerned that she was either ripping them off or that their product was at fault. I'm certainly no advocate of smoking, but this is smart business on behalf of Rothmans. They track their complaints so they can detect trends and also follow up on repeat complaints.

An *American Banker* survey found that the number one reason why people change banks is because of poor service—21 percent leave because of bad service, whereas 12 percent leave to seek higher interest rates (Zemke and Schaaf 1989).

I'm totally convinced that banks don't actually "win" customers until another bank has well and truly "lost" them, as it is quite an arduous task for a customer to change banks. Most won't do so because of some glossy advertising campaign, but because they were thoroughly turned off by their own bank and then a great advertising campaign presented them with a palatable choice.

Most patrons who don't go back to restaurants cite poor service as the reason for not returning (Zemke and Schaaf 1989). One would have thought food would have been the prime reason but, unless the food was particularly poor, service appears to be the deciding factor for diners—78.4 percent of the time individuals dine out, they return to an old standby restaurant.

Some Australian research demonstrates these statistics are not unique to the United States. As quoted in *The Age* (December 18, 1991):

> *More than half of a group of small and medium-sized businesses surveyed by the chartered accounting firm, have considered changing banks because they find the service unsatisfactory. The survey of 100 businesses found 52 percent had thought about changing banks because of inadequate bank customer communication and support and because they believed pricing and security requirements were unrealistic. Only 10 percent of those surveyed used smaller banks and many of those who considered changing banks said they believed smaller banks gave better service. 21 percent had never met or did not know the bank manager and 48 percent said their main contact at the bank did not satisfactorily understand the client business.*

Even though that quote is from 1991, it's still true today. So too, the comments in *The Financial Review* (February 5, 1992):

> *The standard of service from fund managers is as important as the managers' investment success according to a survey by economic forecaster BIS Shrapnel. The statistical survey of more than 500 Australian funds has established a link between qualitative performance and the fund manager's market share. The study also pointed to the link between qualitative performance and the prospects of gaining new business. Stephen Moore, head of the banking and finance unit at BIS Shrapnel said the survey established that those managers who improved the quality of their operations, and the client perceptions of these services, could expect to gain a greater market share.*

I think it's safe to say that service has become, and will continue to become, even more of a differentiating factor.

4 Track records don't count . . . enough!

Customers' perceptions of services provided by organizations are determined to a great extent by the track record that they have established. Naturally, an impressive history of financial stability and customer service is an advantage to any business.

However, it is equally important to remember that track records are not enough to guarantee customer loyalty. As impressive as your track record may be in obtaining a customer in the first place, the customer is more interested in the individual attention received or not received at any particular point in time. It would be of little consolation for a customer to be told: "We're very sorry but that's the first time in the history of our organization that this (unfortunate event) has happened."

Any customer is much more interested in what is personally happening to him or her at any point in time, regardless of how impressive an organization's track record may be.

Also, it is certainly no consolation for a customer to be informed: "Oh don't worry, that (mistake) happens all the time. You're not the only one."

I was speaking to staff at Rich River Golf Club, along the Murray River border between NSW and Victoria. One of the cleaners came up and said he understood exactly what I was talking about when I mentioned track records not being important enough.

"You know, if we have the place sparkling clean, no one notices and thanks us. But, if we miss just one little bit of dirt, everyone seems to notice. It's just not fair."

I agreed with him that it wasn't fair, but such were customer expectations. The "unfair" thing about being a service leader is that the customer comes to take a lot for granted...but also comes back.

"Yep, I guess you're right. I never really thought about it that way before and we're going to have the cleanest golf course in Australia."

5 Anticipate changing market expectations

Naturally enough, customer expectations change. They change not only as the organization changes, but as consumers become more sophisticated and/or other competitive products or services appear in the marketplace. Successful companies will not only be able to cope with change, but will anticipate it and be leaders in initiating it.

After living in Japan and Hong Kong for a couple of years, I returned to Australia with changed expectations of customer service. As delighted as I was to be home, I was appalled with the lack of service provided. Although there were exceptions to this rule, tradespeople were often unreliable and ill equipped, and their work was inadequately done.

I couldn't help but make comparisons with Japan. The Japanese refer to a customer as *o-kyaku-san*, which translates into an "honorable visitor in one's home." This was evident in every aspect of Japanese service that I experienced from the moment of my arrival. For example, when I wanted to get the phone connected, I called and made a request. They asked what time would be convenient to me and then showed up precisely at that time the next day!

I had the same pleasant experience with the gas company and the retailer who installed my stereo. Even groceries were delivered within 15 minutes of the promised time. In Tokyo, Toyota buyers can choose a car and specify any color and features on a Monday and receive that car on a Friday.

It would be far too simple for the reader to dismiss these observations and claim I have unrealistic expectations of service as a result of having had the unique opportunity to live in Japan. This is not to suggest that you should copy Japan!

But trade within the Asia-Pacific region is growing, as is evidence that customer expectations have changed as a result of Asian influence. One simply needs to ask executives of General Motors what Toyota has done to customer expectations in New Zealand. Or, the management of what was once Australia's largest retailer, Myer, to determine how the introduction of the Daimaru department store in central Melbourne has altered customer expectations. Myers, which is located right next door to Daimaru, profited from these increased service standards by improving their own service levels, while having more price-competitive products.

Some of the customer-focused facilities that Daimaru provides are:

- infant changing and feeding facilities for moms and dads, with a microwave oven, playpen, bottle warmer, bath, and baby strollers;
- child care at reasonable rates with a 50 percent discount if the customer spends more than $20;
- powered wheelchairs for elderly or disabled customers to rent;
- parking discounts with every purchase;
- parcel storage lockers;
- bilingual salespeople;
- employees who have received two weeks' training, know the store's products, and are extremely helpful;
- electronic touch computer screens providing information.

A quote in one of Daimaru's promotional brochures sums up the situation:

With six floors packed full of excitement, shopping in Melbourne will never be the same again. That's Fair Dinkum [Australian slang meaning the absolute truth].

I do not for a moment propose that American stores copy the ways of Japan, Australia, or anywhere else! Nor vice versa! That would be a mistake. But as other players influence customer expectations globally, we all need to focus continually on catering to changing customer expectations as the service bar is lifted higher. By doing so, everyone will benefit.

Change is not only culturally driven. The introduction of couriers and fax machines during the 1980s resulted in dramatic improvements in the postal service provided. Likewise, the improvement in telephone service levels has increased dramatically in recent years. With deregulation it is amazing how competition can contribute to improved service. In recent years, itemized accounts have become the norm, and there are choices of varying payment plans, geared to suit consumers' differing requirements.

Other changes have taken place within organizations and in the manner in which customers are served. Also, there is no doubt that the Internet has changed and will significantly continue to change the traditional methods of distribution. Organizations are taking responsibility and following up to see that their customers are served well, and well served.

As well as being influenced by culture and competition, expectations of service are dramatically affected by increasingly sophisticated customers. The increase in consumer education magazines and television programs has created a greater awareness and more informed and demanding customers. What was once considered to be exceptional service may become the norm.

Obviously the discrepancy between what the customer expects and what they perceive is actually delivered results in a happier customer. This is known as "closing the service gap."

About 30 years ago, the State Electricity Commission of Victoria installed power in a small town. After a couple of years, a little old lady wandered into the local SEC office. She thought this newfangled electricity was a wonderful thing and was just wondering when she might "go off probation." The staff was puzzled as she explained she had faithfully paid her bills for two years and now hoped she might be considered worthy to receive power during the day as well as the evening. On further investigation, they learned the power supply to her house had inadvertently been connected to the street lights, so they only came on, when they did, in the evening!

Because the customer had no idea of what realistic service levels to expect, she was quite content with what she received. Can you imagine how irate anyone would be today if the electricity was disconnected for only a few minutes! It all gets back to setting, meeting, and then exceeding customer expectations!

6 Consistency is key

Superior customer service has been defined as "creating predictably positive experiences for customers by consistently meeting and exceeding customer expectations." The two keywords are predictable and consistent. It is relatively easy to give good service on one single occasion, but it takes more effort for organizations to provide consistently positive experiences so that customers keep coming back.

Let me give you an example. On a recent flight I had a dreadful experience with a flight attendant on a well-known carrier. As I was a frequent flier on this airline, I was irate and fully intended to write a letter of complaint but, like most customers, never did. On the return flight on the same airline, I had exactly the opposite experience with a flight attendant who was fantastic. So, it would be easy to rationalize that "on average" my experience with the airline was satisfactory. However, customer service is not about "on average." It's about predictable positive experiences and consistently meeting and exceeding customer expectations.

Tradespeople often advertise their 24-hour services in the Yellow Pages. Using the contact numbers—cell phone, office, or home—the experience is often negative. The cell phone is out of range, the fax screams in your ear, and the answering machine is on. The call is not returned. You are without the service and you won't use that person again.

Let's conclude this chapter on expectations with a few more positive examples.

A colleague told me a story they'd read on the front page of a leading Australian newspaper. It provides a simple example of exceeding customer expectations in a small retail shop.

A customer phoned Tie Rack on Wynyard Station concourse. Would someone meet her at the George Street entrance with a pair of size M tan boxer shorts because she couldn't find parking? And, oh yes, please bring change for $50. The sales assistant found her parked halfway up the footpath and quickly completed the sale.

Another great example of exceeding customer expectations involves the Toyota Lexus. A couple was test-driving a car. The salesman outlined many features and answered all questions, but he spent a great deal of time building rapport with the woman; learning about the children, her taste in music, hobbies, and so on. When the couple took delivery of the car, they were astounded to find $200 worth of her favorite compact discs as a gift. This did a great deal to counter post-sales dissonance and resulted in them telling friends and acquaintances about the great service. Although the actual features of the product they bought may have been somewhat overshadowed, the salesman had certainly succeeded in creating a delighted customer.

This story apparently spread quite rapidly among potential Lexus customers. Many came to "expect" complimentary CDs as part of their purchase. That's what happens when you exceed customer expectations. What was once exceeding expectations becomes the norm, but isn't it better to be exceeding customer expectations than have your competitors do so? And, how much are the CDs worth in comparison with the ongoing customer loyalty and free word-of-mouth advertising?

Customer expectations can be exceeded in the most unusual ways. Midway through a game at Royal Pines, Queensland, a tropical storm hit. Four avid golfers decided to continue and were amazed that, within a few minutes, one of the staff arrived with umbrellas and dry towels for them!

Setting, meeting, and exceeding customer expectations can contribute dramatically to business success. Let's not be like the store that advertises:

> **For the most efficient service, we recommend self-service.**

Rather, let's aim to be like the gas station that "promises good and delivers great" by advertising on their huge signs out front:

> **Full service at self-service prices!**

SEVEN KEY POINTS
in this chapter on exceeding expectations:

1 Set, meet, and then exceed customer expectations to stand out in the marketplace.

2 Customer perceptions of good service contribute directly to the bottom line.

3 Close the gap between what customers expect and what they perceive is being delivered.

4 Track records don't count...enough!

5 Create predictably positive experiences through consistency.

6 Anticipate changing expectations...yesterday's outstanding service is tomorrow's norm.

7 In my own organization, I will improve service through setting, meeting, and exceeding expectations by:

_____

_____

_____

_____

_____

_____

_____

- S ELF—ESTEEM

- E XCEED EXPECTATIONS

3 Recover

- V ISION

- I MPROVE

- C ARE

- E MPOWERMENT

*96 percent of dissatisfied customers
never bother to complain! In other
words, each single customer complaint
represents 24 other people who are equally
unhappy with that good or service . . .
but simply take their business elsewhere.*

1 Complaints are opportunities . . . not problems!

You never get a second chance to make a first impression, but chances are that you *will* get a second chance to make a good impression. Naturally, the smartest strategy is to get it right by the customer in the first place. However, there is usually an opportunity to recover from an error and retain a customer, once you identify the problem.

Technical Assistance Research Programs (TARP) of the U.S. Department of Consumer Affairs in Washington, D.C., provides the alarming statistic that most customers don't bother to complain and simply take their business elsewhere (Albrecht 1990). Statistically, 96 percent of consumers won't complain to the service provider. The 4 percent who do complain are, in fact, your most loyal customers.

This is a clear illustration that no news is not good news. Complaints should be regarded not as a problem, but as an opportunity to fix a situation. Providers of goods and services must be constantly aware of the silent majority and be active in soliciting feedback from this group.

The TARP findings state that the 96 percent of customers who never complain to the service provider do share their experiences with friends and acquaintances.

Each happy customer on average will tell at the most six other people. Each unhappy customer will tell at least 15 other people. It's simply human nature. How often do you tell people when an automatic teller machine works smoothly? Yet, it can work well on hundreds of occasions and the first time it gobbles up your card, you're likely to share your frustration with anyone who cares to listen.

And what happens when you recall a bad service experience on an average of 15 times? It usually becomes exaggerated. Furthermore, acquaintances join in with similar stories relating to that organization and it almost becomes a contest of: "I can beat that horror story."

Obviously, this is not the sort of word-of-mouth advertising that the service provider relishes. Thus, the strategy, if something must go wrong, is to fix it as soon as possible and try to avoid customers retelling the event. Reduce the number of times a customer repeats a story, even within your own organization. If they complain to the front-desk clerk, don't have them also tell the supervisor and then the manager.

Employees should be trained to handle customer complaints to ensure that they realize the importance of adhering to the following steps, combined with their own good judgment, to help defuse potentially hostile customer situations.

2 How to handle customer complaints

Staff should be adequately trained to handle customer complaints. In doing so, ensure they realize the importance of the following steps to take:

- Don't be defensive.
- Be composed at all times.
- Don't take criticisms personally. It's not you the customer is angry with. Try to be objective and put yourself in their shoes.
- Offer an apology even if the disservice is not your fault. "I'm terribly sorry you are so upset" does not admit blame but does establish some rapport with the customer.
- Show empathy by using such phrases as: "I can understand how you feel," "I appreciate what you're saying."
- Address customers by name.
- All communication should be in the first person. Use: "I am sorry" not the royal "We."
- Don't make excuses or blame others in your organization. The customer wants a solution to their problem, not an inquisition of your internal operations.
- Give the customer your full attention and establish eye contact. Sympathetic nods help defuse situations, and many customers feel they are receiving a fair hearing if they see someone jotting down a few notes.

- Paraphrase their complaint in your own words to determine whether you have correctly understood the situation. Play the situation back to them to check for understanding: "I just want to check that I have understood you correctly?"
- If you don't know the answer to their problem, don't lie. Adopt the old teaching maxim and admit you don't know, but make a commitment that you will find out and get back to them within a specified time.
- Do call back when you say you will, even if, for some reason, you haven't been able to obtain a satisfactory answer by then.
- Make the customer part of the solution—not part of the problem.
- Tell them what you can do . . . not what you can't do. For example, rather than say: "I'm terribly sorry but you must give seven days' notice to transfer money from a term deposit to a checking account," adopt the following "can do" approach that says the same thing but in a different way: "Yes, I can transfer the money from your term deposit to your checking account, with a slight interest charge of X dollars, since you were unable to provide seven days' notice."
- Find out what it will take to turn their dissatisfaction into satisfaction. Do they want a refund, credit, discount, replacement? Offer a solution and obtain the customer's agreement that this would satisfy the complaint. Ask: "Will this problem be solved if we . . . ?"
- If they agree to that solution, act quickly before they change their mind. If they don't like your solution, ask them what they think is a fair outcome.
- Follow up.
- And remember: You can never win an argument with a customer!

Managers of leading service organizations need a sound understanding of the type of customer complaints received. Rather than have staff protect them from complaints, they encourage involvement in order to fix the problem, because they understand that sometimes staff at the front line may be hamstrung by a procedure that only management can alter.

Managers of most leading hotels respond personally to every customer complaint. Let me give an example of two dramatic contrasts in the way management can handle a complaint.

Some time ago, I wrote two letters on the same day—one to a hotel and another to an airline. The reply from the hotel arrived two days later, specifically addressed the problem I had mentioned, and was signed by the general manager.

The reply from the airline arrived two weeks later, did not address the problem I specifically mentioned, and was simply a form letter, signed by the assistant manager of their regional office. It's obvious to see the difference and know which reply was most satisfactory to me.

Undoubtedly, there are instances where a complaint is not even acknowledged.

Respond to each and every complaint. If a busy person takes the time to write a letter of complaint, then it's important! Make sure you thoroughly investigate all the specifics of the complaint before responding.

A colleague who seldom complains was prompted to write to a hotel outlining her dissatisfaction. They responded promptly, but a typing error addressed her as Mr. instead of Ms., which further exasperated her to the point she will no longer stay at that hotel.

3 Find out what your customers really think—surveys, focus groups, mystery shopping

Many times organizations may welcome customer complaints, but the customers can't be bothered creating a hassle. For example, how many times has a waiter or waitress asked: "How's your meal?" and you simply responded: "Fine, thanks"?

That's a standard response to a standard question, even if the meal was bordering on mediocrity . . . or worse. Would you have been more likely to offer some suggestion if they had asked: "Is there anything we could have done to have made your meal more enjoyable?" or "Would you have the minestrone again?"

These open-ended questions are less threatening and, chances are, you may have been more forthcoming with suggestions. More useful questions in this regard are those such as:

"how may I help you?"

"how might we have done better?"

Service-focused organizations go out of their way to solicit customer comments and then act on those suggestions. They recognize that customer service is not the prerogative of the customer complaints department but involves every employee in the organization. If they have a customer complaints desk, they rotate personnel from that position to keep them fresh and also to give all employees an opportunity to gain first-hand exposure to what customers really think of the organization. If complaints are left to the customer relations department who never sees customers, this implies no one else in the organization is responsible for customer relations.

The executives of service-focused organizations aren't afraid to get personally involved. Blackmores, the family-founded health and vitamin company, is a profitable business on the Australian stock exchange today. The managing director, Marcus Blackmore, is said to personally call customers who complain. He calls when they are most likely to be home, around 6 p.m. They receive a replacement product and all information received is passed on to the research and development section to improve the products in line with customer suggestions. What's more, when the new products come on the market, a sample is sent to the people whose suggestions resulted in the changes. I understand Blackmores receives many letters of astonishment from customers when this happens. In addition, you can be sure that those amazed customers will not only become more brand-loyal, but will be telling their friends.

Just how important is one single complaint that the CEO feels it is worth chasing up personally? One complaint statistically represents 24 similar ones. Many companies, like Blackmores, compile a long-term database of complaints to determine whether there are any trends.

It's critical to know what your customers are thinking. That's why Gallup polls, television ratings, and political polls are conducted.

Service-focused companies welcome all customer comments. They go out of their way to obtain them. In the United States, the number of toll-free numbers installed is growing 25 percent annually. This makes it easy for customers, at no expense, to complain and offer suggestions to top management. Many of these phone lines are staffed 24 hours a day, seven days a week to make it easy for customers to speak their mind whenever a thought occurs to them . . . or, if they prefer, to send complaints via e-mail.

A number of companies now listen to customers by inviting them (even the unhappy ones) to speak to conferences of employees. It's a gutsy move and management needs to be totally committed to improving service quality, but it is an excellent way for behind-the-scenes employees to discover, firsthand, what the customer is really thinking about the product.

Many organizations send surveys to customers. Most people are too busy to fill them in, but the percentage of responses is often indicative of the feelings of other customers. Some organizations have surveys at the point of sale. Even local gymnasiums have questionnaires on the quality of the workout, asking for suggestions on how the instructor might improve.

Many organizations offer incentives to customers who take the time to give their opinion. Some offer guests an opportunity to win a prize, simply by answering a few questions on a form. It's important to keep the questions to a minimum so the customer can readily see it will only take a short time to respond.

A hotel in Auckland has an excellent incentive to solicit information from its frequent guests. If you fill in their customer satisfaction survey, you receive bonus points on your frequent visitor program, which can be redeemed for free stays.

Focus groups take more time than a survey but can provide more in-depth information on the perception customers have of service provided by an organization. A focus group is simply a collection of a small number of customers who are asked many questions about the organization. Often a response by one participant will trigger responses from others that would not necessarily have emerged from a questionnaire.

Focus groups can be conducted by skilled interview staff or members of your own organization. James Strong, recently retired chief executive officer of Qantas Airlines, in his customer-focused push at the then-Australian Airlines, invited pilots and baggage handlers to have lunch with customers in their own time. This allowed them to hear complaints firsthand as Strong encouraged customers to tell staff exactly what was wrong.

The logic was that a handler who hears firsthand from a customer about baggage problems will have a better understanding of the issue than management and will go back and tell his or her colleagues. This is not only more "real" and believable than some obscure management memo instructing them to fix the problem, but gets people at the front line involved with the organization and provides them with more job satisfaction through an opportunity to make a difference to the overall success of the company.

On one occasion, a handler returned to the baggage room and outlined the customer complaint to his colleagues. As a result, they drew up a plan and wrote to the customer to say what they were going to do about his problem. They then acted upon their plan and made substantial and measurable improvements. What's more, the baggage handlers then wrote to the customer again to say what, in fact, had been done as a result of the customer's input.

That's not to say that the airline will never lose a bag again, but it certainly was a step in the right direction for all customers and employees concerned.

A variation on focus groups is to have an executive sit behind a one-way mirror and hear firsthand what their customers really think of their organization.

"Mystery shopping" is another means by which organizations can find out what really happens at the front line. People can be hired to conduct surprise visits to various locations. Although these mystery shoppers are totally unidentifiable to the person working in the organization, they have a detailed checklist to quantify various levels of good and bad aspects of service delivery. Some organizations will have these mystery shoppers hand out certificates of merit or cash gift vouchers to employees who, they judge, are doing an outstanding job of meeting all the service criteria. Staff are aware that random mystery shopping occurs, but they never know when or where they may be measured, so are attentive to all customers.

4   Test your own service delivery

If you don't want to go to the expense of hiring mystery shoppers with quantitative evaluation forms, it can be equally informative to test your own organization and try your own services from an external customer perspective. Phone in as a customer and see what happens. Was the phone answered promptly and pleasantly? Were you put on hold for an inordinate amount of time? Were you given the runaround? How did you feel after the experience?

The duty manager of Rockmans Hotel in Melbourne calls six to eight customers a day "just to check" that everything is all right and claims: "It's amazing what you find out when you call a guest unexpectedly."

Many organizations ask not only all managers, but all employees, to talk to just one customer per day, week, or month and ask the question: "How can we do better to serve you?"

Other organizations hold mass call days when virtually everyone in the organization goes out to solicit customer opinion and then meets back at the office for a mass review of the findings.

As well as listening to customer complaints, smart management will actively obtain information and suggestions from their employees—many of whom are usually in more direct contact with customers.

In 1984, Toyota in Japan received 1.7 million employee suggestions and implemented 96 percent (Forrest 1987). No wonder they became a threat to U.S. carmakers!

What about customers who complain and are totally incorrect in their complaint . . . or are actually the cause of their complaint? Are these hopeless cases?

The story is told of Armstrong Floors, which showed how to turn such a negative into a positive. It received numerous complaints about its vinyl floor coverings. After the floor was installed for a period, customers complained it didn't look as good as it should and apparently wasn't standing up to the wear and tear as promised. Armstrong knew the real problem was not with the product but with the fact that customers didn't take time to read the care-instruction booklet. They were using abrasive material to clean the floor, which in fact caused the damage. After a great deal of soul-searching, Armstrong came up with the idea of printing a toll-free number on each section of flooring. The customers could not remove this number and each piece of flooring said: "To easily remove this number, call the toll-free number 24 hours a day."

When a customer called, they were told how to remove the number and given two minutes of advice on how to get the most from their new floor. This not only dramatically reduced Armstrong's customer complaints, but also increased rapport and reduced post-sales dissonance between the customer and the supplier.

5 Listen carefully and assume nothing

The importance of careful listening when dealing with customers cannot be overlooked. We are all guilty of occasionally being distracted and paying only partial attention to what people say. That sort of casual listening is a luxury that customer-focused organizations simply cannot afford.

Sydney broadcaster John Raedler tells the story of an interview he did with a 106-year-old man who was born overseas. He asked his producer to check whether the elderly immigrant spoke adequate English to be interviewed. Was he able to walk into studio? Would the excitement of the interview be likely to give him a heart attack? The gentleman's 45-year-old granddaughter assured the producer there was no problem with any of these factors. She brought her grandfather into the studio and sat him down in front of the microphone. When John Raedler asked the first question, there was silence. As a skilled interviewer, he then asked a more open-ended question, only to be greeted by more silence. Only then, on air, did Raedler discover that the gentleman being interviewed was totally deaf. Quickly playing some music, to save further embarrassment, he escorted the elderly gentleman from the studio and asked the granddaughter why she hadn't said he was deaf. Her indignant reply: "You didn't ask *that* question!"

The moral of this story is that we should never assume anything in communications. This point, specifically in relation to customer service, is further illustrated by a leading computer company that regularly conducted customer satisfaction surveys on major customers. One of the factors measured was whether customers were satisfied with the level of preventive maintenance on their mainframes. Preventive maintenance on large computer systems is similar to having a grease and oil change on your car. The system is periodically turned off and the basics checked to avoid a major, unscheduled breakdown.

The six monthly customer survey results showed that customers were "unhappy" with the level of preventive maintenance. Being a customer-focused organization, the computer company formed task forces and went to great lengths to provide more preventive maintenance to their unhappy customers. New and more elaborate procedures were implemented and they were confident the following survey results would show increased customer satisfaction. Much to their dismay, the next survey results indicated the customers were even more unhappy than before, in spite of the efforts that had been made.

It was only on further investigation and in-depth conversation with the customers that the computer company discovered that customers had indicated they were unhappy with the level of preventive maintenance because they wanted less, so their computers would be operating more often! The company had assumed the customers wanted more and thus implemented strategies in exactly the reverse direction to the desired result. Full marks to the company for measuring, responding, and eventually delving deeper into their customer complaints, which were finally resolved to the customers' satisfaction and ended up costing the computer company less money in maintenance on machines.

This same computer company has also learned, the hard way, about the importance of satisfying customer wants, as well as their needs. One of their major customers placed a huge order for a number of machines for their banking network. They asked that the numeral 5 on the keypad be raised to improve teller productivity. As this was not a standard feature on the system, the computer company went to great lengths to prove that a raised number would not, in fact, improve efficiency. After a number of lab visits and research and development studies, the client agreed that they did not need the raised number, but informed the computer company that they wanted it and bought all their equipment from another supplier! Although computer companies were probably guiltier than most in creating customer needs during the 1980s and 1990s, all organizations must be responsive to customer needs and wants in this century.

When listening to customers, it's also important not to dismiss any of their comments as irrelevant. A former chairman of Honda in Japan fully understood the significance of this statement. He personally saw every customer complaint and reply. On one occasion, a woman in the United States complained that a Honda lawnmower was dangerous because it threw up pebbles. Honda engineers were asked to investigate this problem because the company prided itself on safety. The engineers tested the model of lawnmower on grass. They then placed loose pebbles on the grass and there was no problem. To be certain, they further tested the lawnmower on a gravel road and it still didn't throw pebbles, as the customer had complained. The engineers confidently reported to the chairman of Honda that there was no problem with their product and the woman must be incorrect. The sage old chairman listened carefully to their logic and then asked: "But have you tested it on *her* lawn?"

An engineer was flown to the United States and, much to his dismay, discovered that the customer's lawnmower did, in fact, throw pebbles because of a minor problem with an attachment. We can never assume the customer has an irrelevant complaint. We can never assume the complaint results from incorrect equipment use.

Listening to employees is also important. Ken Blanchard, author of *The One Minute Manager*, tells the story of a manufacturing plant that had a 200 percent turnover rate among employees. He was hired as a consultant to fix the problem. Management suggested he talk to various supervisors to determine the key issues, but he insisted on talking to the shop floor personnel. Apparently, within 10 minutes of arriving, the shop floor employees told him: "It's hot as hell down there."

He reported this finding to management, who simply needed to spend a few thousand dollars to install air conditioning, which resulted in significant reductions in staff turnover. The plant could have saved hundreds of thousands of dollars in his fees and previous training of personnel if they had listened to the employees years ago. Apparently, those few, long-serving employees had been telling the foreman for years that heat was the problem.

Listen and learn!

6 When all else fails—how to make amends

As important as it is to avoid errors in the first place, there is still hope to keep a customer if your organization can respond quickly to fixing the problem.

Research from Wharton Business School shows that 95 percent of customers who have a complaint that was handled efficiently and promptly will not only continue to do business with your organization, but will become even more brand-loyal.

The graph from the Wharton Business School demonstrates this point (see Figure 3.1). Do these statistics mean you should get in a mess?

Absolutely not! The 95 percent who become more brand-loyal represent only 4 percent of the people who bothered to complain in the first place. The other 96 percent simply took their business elsewhere or told their friends about the poor service.

Service-oriented organizations need to have every employee focus on the "boomerang benefit" of providing superior service. We want our existing customers to boomerang—to come back—because the TARP shows that it costs five times more to obtain a new customer than to retain an existing one (Albrecht1990)! It is critical that everyone in an organization understands the important role they play in retaining existing customers. Service is not just the responsibility of frontline personnel. All people behind the scenes need to understand the vital role they play. Whether it be the manufacture or delivery of goods, provi-

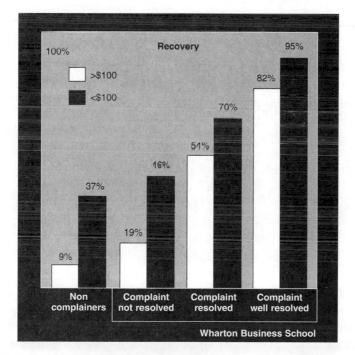

FIGURE 3.1   Complaint resolution results.

sion of accurate customer statements, or maintaining human resource practices to keep employees happy—these factors contribute to having customers boomerang by avoiding complaints in the first place.

If complaints do occur, the key is to handle the complaint satisfactorily and as thoroughly and promptly as possible. Many organizations will not only fix the immediate complaint, but give the customer something extra, in the form of compensation, to apologize for any inconvenience.

Here are some examples of recovery:

- A friend returned a faulty video player to a department store. The salesperson didn't even look in the box but apologized, replaced it with another, and gave her two free videocassettes for the inconvenience.
- Another person ordered a case of wine from Tyrells. On opening the case he found one bottle had been broken. He reported it but he couldn't prove if it was the wine company's fault, the delivery truck's fault, or whether one of his kids had jumped on the box. However, he was pleasantly surprised when he was given an order number to obtain two replacement bottles. This wine tasting buff now claims to be a loyal Tyrells' customer.

When staying at a Sydney hotel on one occasion, I was reminded of the British television comedy *Fawlty Towers*. My telephone didn't function properly, messages weren't received—and they double-booked my room. After I was in bed, a male guest opened the door to the same room. Neither of us was amused. I was dead tired and decided not to bother complaining then as I simply wanted to sleep. However, I did mention it the next morning, as it was certainly not the standard of service I had come to expect from that normally excellent chain.

To cut a long story short, they had some electronic malfunction that had affected the phones and booking system. As I was a frequent visitor to the hotel, they were most apologetic. Much to my surprise, I received a letter from the manager a few days later. He apologized for the inconvenience, admitted there was nothing he could do to rectify the lost messages or disturbed sleep, but hoped I would be able to bring three friends as his guests for dinner one evening. As you can imagine, I still enjoy staying there. There is a risk that customers could use these recovery stories against companies to get free goods. Customers could complain about things that were, in fact, not at all true. It is a risk, but it is a minimal one and the word-of-mouth advertising from happy customers would far outweigh those who may try to rip you off.

Smart companies keep records of customer complaints to monitor those who may be taking unfair advantage of a company's goodwill. But, if even 1 percent of customers may take advantage of the situation, does that mean you should not trust the other 99 percent?

Nordstrom, a retail service leader in the United States, has been known to refund a customer for a product that the store had never even stocked. How can they afford to do this? Very simply, they just take the expense out of their advertising budget. They allow for 1 to 2 percent of customers taking advantage of their goodwill but know the majority, who have their complaints satisfied, will become more brand-loyal and provide invaluable word-of-mouth advertising.

Here are some more recovery stories that may or may not be relevant to your organization:

- A New Zealand tour company had supplied incorrect directions to a ski lodge, which resulted in our driving around needlessly in the middle of the night. What's more, the car provided at the airport did not have snow chains and a ski rack, in spite of written confirmation, which wasted another hour getting these fitted. It was not a great start to a holiday and we were not amused. I complained and didn't think any more about it, because I must admit the rest of the vacation was excellent. On returning home, we were feeling pretty positive about the tour company, especially when there was a letter of apology and refund for one day's car rental.
- A friend was shipping some goods to Malaysia and was promised delivery within six weeks. When she had not received them after two months, she phoned me in Sydney to follow up on the shipment. It was discovered the goods were still sitting in Australia. Apparently, she had received a quote based on a full container load and the supplier was still waiting until some other shipment could make up a full container. They readily agreed they should have notified her of the delay and sent the goods by air at their expense.

■ A postal worker in Tamworth, New South Wales, was unable to deliver the mail on Christmas Eve because of a flat tire on his truck. Not to be deterred, he went home later that evening and drove his own vehicle to get the mail through.

And, this is probably my favorite, kindly supplied to me by Graham Street, the former technical manager for Philips in New Zealand. Figure 3.2 is an excerpt from an actual complaint letter,

June 14, 1999

The Manager
Philips
PO Box 1041
Mt Albert

RE: Philips Filterline Type HD4601/A Batch No: 9638

Dear Sir/Madam:

We purchased our Automatic Teakettle from "Company X," which has since closed down, and have had nothing but trouble with it since we've had it.

It has never worked properly and started playing up shortly after purchase. It would not stay on and we had to play with it to get it to work at all—*a bit like my husband really—but we won't go there!*

We have another old teakettle so we took the new one in to be repaired—copy of the invoice enclosed.

Alas, this was not to be, as it never worked properly when we had it back. We took it back and they mended it again—no charge but it came back just the same, broken!—not having time to pursue this we sat it on the bench looking good for a few weeks before we relegated it to the teakettle graveyard. But would you believe the old teakettle has packed up and we now find it necessary to purchase yet another teakettle—I should state that we are English and can't survive without a good drop of the Earl Grey!

Please advise us what to do, is it worth getting another Philips or will we have the same problem?

We are not going to have ours repaired again—it obviously has an attitude problem and is the Black Sheep of teakettles and will never change its boiling point!

FIGURE 3.2   Copy of complaint letter

the name and address of the customer obviously deleted. And after fixing the problem, with the sense of humor such a letter would warrant, Figure 3.3 is the certificate of appreciation that the customer sent back. And as you can imagine, they bought many more Philips products for themselves and as gifts for their family.

Another example from this same service champion at Philips also caught my attention. He'd received an e-mail at 4:07 p.m. on August 4 regarding a complaint about the battery life of an electric toothbrush. At 5:09 he replied that a replacement had been sent. The original complaint e-mail had gone from New Zealand to Europe to the regional office in Singapore, back to the local office in New Zealand in less than two hours, where Graham Street thought he would surprise the customer by putting the part in the mail on his way home from work so it arrived as soon as possible. The sequence of events is shown in Figure 3.4.

FIGURE 3.3   Certificate of appreciation

FIGURE 3.4   Customer complaint resolution

To: AKL/DAP/PHILIPS
cc: feedback
Subject: NEW_ZEALAND - GENERAL
Time: 4.07 pm. NZ   Date: August 4

Company:
Name: Customer X

Comments:
Having used Philips products for more than 30 years, I'm very disappointed
with the hp735/a Toothbrush purchased in September. It no longer works.
Could be a battery problem, but a nickel cadmium surely should last longer
than this?? Makes brushing one's teeth a very expensive deal!

(a) E-mail to Philips (International Office) from Customer X

To: Graham Street
cc:
Subject: NEW_ZEALAND - GENERAL
Time: 4.30 pm. NZ   Date: August 4

Please help this disgruntled Philophile!!!!!

Thanks
AKL/DAP

(b) E-mail within Philips (on the same day)

To: Customer X
cc:
Subject: HP735
Time: 5.09 pm. NZ   Date: August 4

Ref your e-mail, replacement HP735 hand piece in mail today. No the fault
is not due to nickel cadmium batteries.

Regards, Graham Street

(c) Reply to customer (again on the same day)

06 August 1999.

Mr G Street,
Philips New Zealand Ltd.,
P O Box 1041,
AUCKLAND.

Dear Graham,

Re: My Email yesterday afternoon concerning Faulty Model HP735/A

I received your Email response only a couple of hours later and appreciated the speedy action.

Then, to my utter amazement, [and please excuse my astonishment – one doesn't expect this sort of service these days, even from a Company like Philips] in my P O Box this morning, was the replacement for our faulty unit!

Having been in the service industry for 35 years, I fully appreciate the value and importance of good service - but this effort deserves a place in the "Guinness Book of Records".

Whatever culture, attitude, service levels, etc. an organisation has as its goals, a company is only as good as its people.

I congratulate you and thank you for this example of unsurpassed customer service.

I have had good value from the many Philips products purchased over the past 30-odd years and look forward to continuing my patronage for the next 30   if I live that long!

Finally, if I am any judge of people and their work ethic, which having been CEO of two National Companies I claim to so be, this letter will [I sincerely hope] bring you some personal satisfaction - but will then get 'filed'.

Please do not do this – I specifically request that you copy this letter to your Manager.

You deserve proper recognition for this and, since it will not be an isolated incident, the obviously regular high standard of performance you contribute to a fine old Company.

The faulty unit is returned herewith as requested.

With Kind regards and Best Wishes.

Yours sincerely,

Customer X

MANAGING DIRECTOR

(d) Letter from customer

To: Customer X
cc:
Subject: Thanks
Time: Date: August 9

Dear Customer X
Thanks for your letter and comments received last Friday. It was a pleasant surprise to receive the compliments. As I am an old hand in the industry going back to the days when I worked for PYE in Waihi, I know the importance in looking after your customer, as it is The Customer who pays the Salary, not the employer.

Recently I met an interesting presenter from Australia called Catherine DeVrye, who also runs seminars on Good Customer Service. So to receive your letter only confirms how important your team, culture, and attitudes are.

Yes, I did pass a copy onto my Manager. (Who wants it now for future reference.)

Finally, the new technology & tools are a great thing. When you sent your message, it went to Philips in Eindhoven, then back to our regional office in Singapore and finally the local office in Auckland to look after the customer's needs. All of this within 2 hours. As the local mail had been collected when your message came in, I thought I would surprise the customer and post it at the South Auckland Mail Centre on my way home from work.

Once again thanks,
regards,
Graham Street
Technical Manager, Domestic Appliances & Personal Care.

(e) **Follow-up email**

To: Graham Street
cc:
Subject: Re: Thanks
Time: 10 am   Date: August 10

Graham,

As you say, the wonders of modern science!

However, these, like any facilities, are only as good as THE PEOPLE
who work with them.

Excellent Facilities + Poor People still = Bad Result.
Any Facilities + Good People = The Best result possible.

Your extra effort and thoughtfulness brought the best result possible for
this very happy customer.

Thanks again.

Customer X

p.s. the replacement is very good and seems of far sturdier construction.

(f) Reply from customer

Wow—wouldn't you like a letter like that from a customer?
Wouldn't you like employees like that? Now, I'm not in a position to
endorse Graham Street or Philips or any other product because
undoubtedly some reader may have a not so favorable story about the
same company; but I have the original documentation to substantiate
these two case studies and we all know that any service from any
company is only as good as you get at that particular point in time.
But these two examples don't get much better, and the gentleman
concerned seems a true gentleman in every sense of the word and
goes that extra mile to delight customers.

He, and I'm sure countless other service champions around the
world, recognize that customer complaints can be a headache or a
delight, depending on how you look at them. But, if you don't know
what the problem is, you've got no chance of fixing it.

Do it now. Be active and avoid any time-consuming investigations by departments of consumer affairs or ombudsmen. It's too late and costly to recover at that stage.

Look at what you can do to turn every customer problem into an opportunity!

An outstanding recovery story comes from an American visiting Tokyo. He bought a compact disk player at Odakyu Department Store. He didn't open the package until the next morning and found that it didn't work. He was waiting to call the store when it opened at 10 a.m. but at 9:59 the store called him. The vice-president of the store was on his way over with a new compact disk player. A taxi pulled up and the vice-president and a young employee emerged and bowed repeatedly.

The young man read from a log that outlined their efforts to rectify the error beginning at 4.32 p.m. the previous day when the sales clerk realized his error and alerted store security to stop the customer at the door. When that didn't work, he turned to his supervisor who went up the ladder to the vice-president, working on the only clue they had-an American Express number. The clerk called 32 hotels in Tokyo and then stayed until 9 p.m. to call American Express in New York. They gave him the customer's New York number and the people at the house gave him the number in Tokyo. By this time, it was after 11 p.m. so they waited until morning to call the customer.

As well as the new compact disk player, the customer received a set of towels, a box of cakes, and a Chopin compact disc. The vice-president continued to apologize, saying he hoped the visiting American customer would understand that it was the young man's first day on the job!

S E V E N   K E Y   P O I N T S
in this chapter on recovery:

1 96 percent of unhappy customers never complain—to you. They tell others and go elsewhere.

2 Complaints are opportunities—not problems.

3 It's your most loyal customers who complain and word-of-mouth advertising is powerful in the marketplace.

4 Don't wait for customers to tell you about their problems. Ask them first.

5 Appreciate the boomerang benefits of good service and adopt a "can do" approach to every situation.

6 You can never win an argument with a customer.

7 In my own organization, I will improve service recovery by:

_____

_____

_____

_____

_____

_____

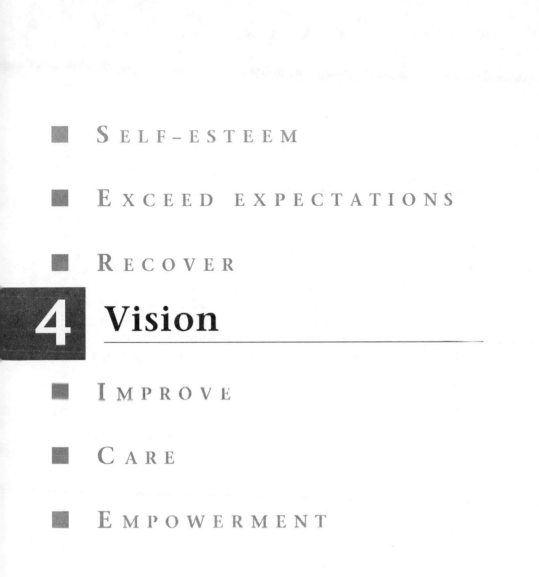

■ SELF-ESTEEM

■ EXCEED EXPECTATIONS

■ RECOVER

4 Vision

■ IMPROVE

■ CARE

■ EMPOWERMENT

*Do you have the facts and figures
on the lifetime value of your customers?*

> . . . You can't drive into
> the future using a
> rearview mirror.

1 Plan for the future today!

Leaders need a vision of what superior service looks like in their organization—not only today, but in years to come. They must be able not only to cope with changes in consumer behavior, but to anticipate and welcome those changes. Leaders may, at times, seem a bit radical to others who don't dare to share the vision for the future.

Look at the Sydney Opera House. It's hard to believe that there were so many controversies that surrounded its construction at the time it was first built. Can anyone imagine Sydney without it today?

Times change and so do opinions and consumer patterns. Can you imagine trying to explain "smart" cars or "thinking" refrigerators to our great grandparents, who never even owned the "dumb" models? Successful organizations not only cope with change, but are able to anticipate it. In 1972 even distinguished academics would have thought you were crazy if you told them a female would become prime minister of the U.K. Or that 60 percent of wine sold would be in cardboard boxes. Common usage words like "multicultural," "globalization," "privatization," and "triathlon" weren't even in the spellchecker of my word-processing package, just before the turn of the century—and I mean the 20th century! Even a few years ago, any responsible adult would have been worried about a child who wanted to be a Web master when they grew up!

What does all this futuristic stuff have to do with service, you may ask? We've moved from an industrial revolution to an information revolution and are progressing toward a service revolution. Many companies are in both the information and service sectors, and provision of superior service becomes more critical as industries mature.

Global business is no longer an esoteric term or one reserved for big multinationals. Twenty-four hours a day, 365 days of the year, customers can access Web sites, which substantially reduces the tyranny of distance for businesses not "centrally" located next to major markets. You can respond to inquiries from your office, home, or plane. But even if you are 30,000 feet in the air, it's important to keep your feet firmly on the ground and recognize that if you're a small operation, it's not always realistic to respond in real time to an inquiry from the other side of the world.

Your competition may now only be a mouse click away and even though you sometimes feel like a mouse trapped in a technology maze, it's unlikely you'll ever get the cheese if you don't first recognize the rapid changes that could result in you following a different direction.

As futurist Joel Barker states: "We'd better pay attention to the future because that's where we're going to spend the rest of our lives."

It's critical to plan for the future of your company. It's important to have a positive vision of that future especially in tough times. A vision, accompanied by a sound plan of action, can produce lasting results.

It's not unusual for Japanese companies to have 50- or 100-year plans, unlike Western firms that base their outlooks solely on annual results. A Japanese construction company, Shimizu, has announced it intends to open a hotel in outer space by 2020. That *is* a challenge for the services sector!

Then again, it's possible to plan too far out and be inflexible to rapid changes happening today. After a seminar in Sydney, *In Search of Excellence* author Tom Peters told me that in Silicon Valley, some successful company's idea of long-term planning is a few weeks out, as change is happening so quickly.

It's not at all unusual for high-tech companies to reject the commonly embraced notion of long-term planning that was popular when computers first entered the workplace. Now, many information technology firms may alter their strategic plans on a monthly or even a weekly basis in an attempt to keep up with the Web speed at which the world is now operating. Rather than worry about keeping up with the Joneses, we'll worry about keeping up with the Webbses!

Thirty years ago, it was big companies versus small; now it seems to be the quick and the slow—or the quick and the dead, depending on your industry.

Who knows any exact time frame on a vision? But make sure you never lose sight of yours—at any time.

It's unrealistic to even try and predict all the necessary changes required in business and beware of those who profess to do so. Any adult pretending to have all the answers shouldn't be allowed in public without supervision! Nor should anyone unwilling to keep asking the questions.

I honestly don't even know if you'll be reading this book in the traditional way or downloading it on to your cell phone by the time of the next reprint. But, I do know that leaders need vision. Managers can simply administer the rules. In every mission statement, leading companies are increasingly referring to service as part of their long-term vision. It is not the intent of this book to discuss mission statements in any depth. Suffice it to say that service must be integrated into the long-term vision for the company, simply because it pays to do so, even if the length of a long-term vision is becoming shorter with Web speed in some industries.

2   Calculate the lifetime value of customers

Do you have the facts and figures on the lifetime value of your customers?

It's important to look not only at the customer of today, but what that customer, their family, and their friends will be worth to you over a long period.

A store that sells only poultry, dairy products, and fresh produce collected statistics that showed the average customer spends $100 per week over a 10-year average life cycle. That amounts to $50,000 in a decade, and the owner encourages employees to visualize every customer walking through the store with $50,000 plastered on their forehead, because that's what he feels they are actually worth (Zemke and Schaaf 1989).

This value is substantially more than the cost of a carton of milk. One customer returned a carton of milk, claiming it was sour. The salesperson inspected the product and assured the customer there was no problem. The owner overheard this and apologetically handed the customer not one, but four, cartons of milk. He then explained to the salesperson that even though she was right, it simply wasn't worth arguing with the customer and emphasized that each customer was worth $50,000 over a lifetime.

This retailer also has one of the lowest advertising budgets of similar dairy stores. Their word-of-mouth customer advertising saves them money in the long term.

One of the most successful automobile dealers in the United States during the 1990s calculated that the average customer spends $142,000 with him. This isn't a rough estimate but based on statistics collected on index cards over the years. He uses that information intelligently. Not only does he know the buying patterns of customers, but also keeps data on their interests, likes and dislikes, and family members. When a customer's child is about to turn 16 (the legal driving age in most states in the United States), he calls up and advises the customer that he's just acquired a car that would probably be perfect for a first car. Now, it would be easy to argue that index cards are old fashioned and you could keep much better records on an electronic database, but the point is that it worked for this car salesman because he used the information.

Without focusing too much on those two examples, look at it this way. How much are you worth to Company X over a lifetime, even assuming you are likely to move to a different geographic location every 10 years?

For example, if you are worth only two suits a year to a clothing store over a 10-year span, at $400 per suit, that equals $8,000. If you tell only one other person, they're also worth $8,000. But, the likelihood is that you will tell six others, which would result in $48,000 to the store over that time.

So, if a frontline salesperson is responsible for a portfolio of $48,000 based on one encounter with you, shouldn't that person be authorized or empowered to spend $10 on "free" alterations?

The proprietor of the shop where I buy my freshly squeezed orange juice every morning fully comprehends this concept. Eddie always greets me with a smile, a cheery comment, and the occasional joke as he squeezes my $2 glass of orange juice. I'm not a morning person, but he always gets my day off to a good start with his cheerfulness. Some time ago a competitor opened only a few shops away. They were selling exactly the same orange juice for $1.80. Over a period of a year, that would be worth $48.00 to me. That would buy a couple of dozen golf balls so it seemed a sensible decision to make the switch, especially at the rate I lose golf balls!

But, I didn't! Eddie's friendly smile *every* day was worth far more than 20 cents a day for a few golf balls I'd periodically lose anyway. Incidentally, the competition raised their prices to his level a few weeks later as they were simply undercutting to get into the market. And guess what? There's still a line of people at Eddie's each morning.

Eddie has never been to business school or attended a customer service training course, but he fully understands the simple formula of treating customers like long-term appreciating assets. He clearly focuses on repeating his service success each and every day and as a result has a viable, long-term business.

You can use this formula with whatever customer group you wish to, from purchasers of major household appliances to buyers of the lowest ticket items.

The same can be said of our hairdressers, doctors, dentists, bookstores, and so on. It applies whenever we buy dishwashers, dog food, televisions, toothpaste, jeans, or jackhammers.

Data from the Australian Bureau of Statistics indicates that the average weekly household expenditure on common items—as found in the table below. Assuming a customer does business with one supplier

TABLE 4.1   Average weekly household expenditure

Item	Average weekly expenditure*	Average annual expenditure	Average decade expenditure
Dry cleaning	0.65	33.80	338.00
Female hairdressing	1.90	98.80	988.00
Bread	4.73	245.96	2459.60
Female clothing	10.44	542.88	5428.80
Motor vehicle gas and oil	25.57	1329.64	13296.40
Meals out/ carryout	29.49	1533.48	15334.80

—Source: Household Expenditure Survey: Details Expenditure Items 1993–94.
Australian Bureau of Statistics, Cat. No. 6535.0.

for 10 years, the figures dramatically show the long-term value of repeat business. (Although these particular extrapolations are based on Australian dollars and data, the same principle holds true whether we're talking U.S. dollars, British pounds, or Japanese yen.)

After I'd spoken at a hairdressing conference, a young woman came up and told me an exceptional story of her long-term vision for her newly found business.

> *My salon is in the city and there are a lot of single people who always tell me they have trouble meeting others, so I decided to invite 40 of my favorite customers to a Valentine's Day party. I figured if even a handful of them fell in love, they'd be loyal for life. What's more, I'd get the booking to do the hair for the wedding and then their kids. I actually knew all of their likes and dislikes because most of them talk to me so was able to match people up quite well. No weddings yet but one engagement and everyone had a great time and business is booming.*

And, of course in this age of e-commerce, technology can help fine-tune customer information to a level never before imagined with the use of intelligent systems. For example, a retailer no longer needs to check the shelves to see if toilet paper is out of stock. That happens automatically and the order is immediately processed by the wholesaler. But let's imagine for some reason there's been a lot of green and white toilet paper used. Intelligent systems can also project reasons why that may be—maybe for Christmas or St. Patrick's Day, to use a far-fetched example.

What's more, retail technology can help predict buying patterns and potential problems in the future. Let's say that the manufacturer of toilet paper is embroiled in a strike at the paper mill or the forest where one of their key suppliers sources the timber has been devastated by fire. The system would then alert the retailer to consider making plans now to source elsewhere in a few months' time, in anticipation of delivery problems in the supply chain. This is very much the bare essentials overview, if you can excuse the pun!

An entrepreneur friend of mine and former IBM colleague puts it very well when he talks about the mobility of service. For example, at the moment if your PC or washing machine breaks down, you need to call a service center to have it repaired. Wouldn't it be more convenient if the diagnostics were built in and you could actually be alerted in advance of a part wearing out or malfunction? Even if it did happen, the information on what part was required and what sort of specialized expertise was required would automatically be recorded so the repairperson could come to your home with all the relevant parts without having to hold inventory or wait for a delivery. And, you'd let them know via e-mail or voice mail what time was convenient to you to have the equipment replaced. This all sounded pretty good to me as John Richards, CEO of QSI, went on to explain that we're not really talking about computers when we're talking about the future of technology and services, but talking about "appliances" with information access; again to save the end-user time through a multidimensional service that coordinates every event along the way that is required to reach a successful outcome, while maintaining strict security of data.

What's more, the service provider, when visiting the home or the office, has more information at their fingertips to put them in a position to up sell. For example, they might look at my laptop computer and see it's an ancient (almost two years old!) model that is heavier than the state-of-the-art laptops. They'd know from my usage report that I log on to my e-mail from various points around the world so they're in a stronger position to convince me of the benefits of buying a smaller and lighter machine, especially if they guaranteed they'd transfer all the data seamlessly so I wouldn't have to spend time doing so. Time and time again . . . saving time is the essence of service in most industries today . . . unless of course, you want a nice long relaxing massage.

Or if I obtain cash from the ATM, the bank would have more information on my spending patterns and might offer me exclusive tickets to an upcoming sporting or musical event, for which I'd simply need to key in my pin number and out would come the ticket or confirmation of my seating. I may not have even been aware the event was on, but they made it so easy for me to spend the money that I'm likely to be happy to do so and see it as a value-added service.

The service provider is actually solving my problem of upgrading my PC or obtaining tickets, before I even knew I was likely to have a problem or that I wanted tickets!

The Internet can also raise revenue for time-sensitive products. It allows airlines and hotels to fill otherwise unused seats and rooms, and the client benefits by obtaining a substantial discount if they have flexibility with their time.

Other organizations are offering significant savings and incentives for clients to "do it themselves" with bookings on the Internet. I think this is indeed an interesting concept with much potential and not all that different to what was once considered the radical introduction of supermarket shopping; to replace the old-fashioned way of being served the groceries from behind the counter or having the shop deliver them to your door in the "old days." They're also now being delivered to your door in the "new days" with online grocery shopping.

Where will this new view of service end up in the future? Or, is it back to the future with the reintroduction of some old-fashioned services via new-fangled means? For your particular business, I guarantee that your guess is better than mine or anyone else's. The sheer rate of growth of the Internet makes it near impossible to accurately predict. According to the June 20, 1999 Washington Post, every second, another seven people around the world tap in for the first time. Look at the trends and decide what's right for your unique circumstances.

And in this information age, try to keep your head above water and don't drown in information and be thirsting for knowledge. Or as a farmer friend would say . . . Be able to sort the wheat from the chaff.

The benefit of having a long-term vision of customers is illustrated by Frederick Recihheld, vice president at Bain & Co.

> *Increasing customer retention by five percentage points can raise the expected lifetime value of a customer from 2-30 percent on the low end and to nearly 100 percent on the top end, depending on the industry.*

> *What explains this dramatic impact on profit? Very simply, the more times customers come back, the more efficient they are to serve. Mature customers tend to buy more. So, with high retention rates you'll have older customers with higher revenues per capita. And, loyal customers are less price-sensitive.*

> —(Zemke and Schaaf 1989)

3 Make technology work for you—not against you

Organizations are naturally concerned about the proliferation of e-mail as there is no longer a "gatekeeper" to control what information leaves the organization. Some companies have limited e-mail access for certain hours in the day so that employees can focus on what they have on their priority "to do" list, rather than continually be in response mode to new e-mails. There are pros and cons to such an approach, but the main thing to remember is that just because e-mail gets out of control, it doesn't mean you need to be! Make sure you manage it as the valuable tool it is, rather than let it manage you.

Technology can certainly assist in retaining loyal, long-term customers if used as a tool to help the customer.

There are many stories about how technology has hindered, rather than helped, customer relations.

"The computer is down."

This catch phrase has replaced the excuse of the check being in the mail. It is a weak excuse to explain some deficiency in service provision. And, although there is no doubt that the computer being down can indeed have a huge impact your service delivery, it's important to be able to look for alternative ways of providing that service, in a "techno emergency." And, believe me, I fully understand the stress—as it's happened to me more than once, when I'd promised someone something and couldn't access e-mail from my hotel room. After stressing out for a couple of hours, I simply had to phone the client and say I was sorry that I couldn't provide what I promised within the time frame because my modem was somehow incompatible with the hotel switchboard, and would it be okay if I sent the information in the mail to arrive a couple of days later? The client was satisfied with that solution (as it had happened to him as well). And, by my being proactive and immediately outlining the problem and resetting the client's expectation *before* the promised time frame had come and gone—and offering the best available alternative—the client was satisfied and not angry. Technology is only as good as its operators—garbage in equals garbage out.

Investing in costly technology won't necessarily make you more profitable or efficient unless it is in line with customer expectations.

In his book *Megatrends*, John Naisbitt outlines a trend from high tech to high touch. Very simply, he states that people are not necessarily overawed by the wizardry of "high technology" and may prefer the old-fashioned "high touch" approach of good old-fashioned customer service. For example, the introduction of automatic teller machines was a dismal failure in a number of retirement communities. Many elderly people found the equipment "unfriendly" and since they generally had more time on their hands than the average customer, they wanted the opportunity to have a chat with a human teller. Combine the high tech with the old-fashioned high touch. Combine the head and the heart for outstanding results.

Recognize customer needs. That is the first step to effective service.

People dealing with customers and using technology should not focus more on the machines than the person being served. Eye contact, a smile, and calling people by name win support. That's far more important than having your head buried in a pile of forms or efficiently staring into a computer screen with glazed eyes. Many organizations have yet to acknowledge this.

British Airways discovered the truth of this statement. As it was striving to improve its reputation among customers, new computer systems were installed to reduce waiting times at check-in, as this was a common complaint area. Check-in agents were instructed to move the customers quickly and not engage in idle chitchat while customers were waiting in a line.

British Airways was horrified, when it surveyed customers a few months later, to find that customers were more unhappy with the service received at check-in, even though they were, in fact, being processed faster than before. To improve the situation, British Airways made two minor modifications. First, they tilted the computer screens to a 45-degree angle. Check-in clerks no longer looked straight down, but their eye level was closer to that of the customer.

Second, the check-in clerks were no longer measured purely on the volume of passengers they "processed" per hour; but on customer satisfaction levels in terms of whether they "felt" they were treated in a friendly way.

British Airways also put on extra staff to check-in customers so passengers scored the double benefit of shorter lines and friendlier service. Although this cost money in the initial stages, it was one of the factors contributing to increased revenues for the airline over the long term.

I was once booked to fly from Auckland to Los Angeles and contacted Air New Zealand as I'd heard on the radio that there was some strike action planned and I wanted to confirm flight departures wouldn't be affected. Not surprisingly, I was immediately greeted by a recorded message. What did surprise me was the timeliness of it and the way in which it immediately set my expectations. It went something along the lines of:

Thank you for calling Air New Zealand. We're sorry to keep you waiting due to an unusually high number of calls as a result of a problem with one of our competitors. (gotcha!) The waiting time is approximately four minutes but we know your time is valuable and if you'd prefer to call back later, we understand.

I decided to wait as I figured the waiting period may be even longer if I called later. Being the sort of person I am, I immediately glanced at my watch and began timing the wait. Would it really be four minutes or five or six or . . . ? Much to my surprise, in less than three minutes my inquiry was readily answered and I complimented the person in the call center for the way in which they had first set and then exceeded customer expectations, rather than the customer making a decision about whether to wait or not, with no idea if they'd be waiting four minutes or four hours.

And one doesn't need to be a huge, elaborate call center to similarly set expectations. When I first started my business, I couldn't afford a secretary so when I was in a meeting, on a plane, or speaking at a conference, all calls would automatically divert to my cell phone. Each day I would update the message with the date and mention of any times that I would be unavailable and an approximate time of when I'd be able to return their call. This gave the caller at the other end some confidence that I wasn't out of town for a week or would simply get back to them when I felt like it.

Friends and clients alike would comment: "How do you find time to do it? Don't you ever forget?" At first I put a note in my diary every day but soon it simply became a habit and, just as I brush my teeth before going to bed every night, so too I automatically update my message, assuming the phone is in range to do so.

Cell phones are now a relatively common technology changing on almost a daily basis. When doctors or airlines know they're going to be running behind schedule, through an emergency or weather condition that may be outside their control, surely they could still have the ability to automatically alert customers to give them a choice to more productively use that time.

Time. Time. There's that word again. We're all time poor. It's the champagne and caviar of this century—the one luxury they're not making any more of and we all wish we had more of. And, anything you can do to give your customers more time will be seen as giving value to them and adding value to your own business.

I laughed at an ad in the paper for a handyman service that read: "I can do almost anything your husband can do around the house—only I'll do it NOW."

Admittedly sexist in nature, that amusing comment again sums up the importance of time and thus the growth in the service industry of such companies as "Wife without strings," "Handy hubby," or mobile dog washing vans. The list is endless and growing.

Call centers and help desks are also meant to save time, but one sometimes wonders if it's to save the customer time or the organization time? Unfortunately, some help desks are helpful in name only, and the people on the end of the phone are not inclined to be helpful at all if your question deviates in the slightest from their pre-prepared script. A good script is essential—like in a great play or movie—but at help desks every character must realize they have an important part to play. Although it's necessary for them to know their lines, it's also sometimes necessary for them to ad lib a little or bring an extraordinary matter to the immediate attention of the director or producer.

Some call centers I find extraordinarily efficient and useful. Because I've already keyed in some of my essential details, like my pin number or account code, the person on the other end of the phone already has a great deal of information, which saves me time having to give my address details or spell my name (and with a name like DeVrye, this can take time!).

Certainly there are some concerns about privacy of client profiles, (and just how much information Big Brother does know about you) but many of these issues, if not already addressed, are close to being so.

It's not within the scope of this book to address the pros and cons of shopping or banking on the Net. Suffice to say, these are now viable choices for those who wish to be served in that manner. And, by the way, if you're anywhere on this planet you can order this and my other books and tapes from my Web site listed at the back of this book. Or, book me to tailor a special message for your next conference.

Also, if you provide a name, I'd be happy to personally inscribe a book for you or one of your friends, customers, or colleagues. Now, this may sound a bit like a "commercial" for the book, but it's just a simple way of illustrating the concept of mass personalization. Mass personalization is another catchphrase of technology, and although it sounds a paradox in terminology, like time, it is something many people value with certain products and services.

Levi Strauss was one of the first to introduce this concept to retailing whereby an electronic tape measure took your precise body measurements and for an extra $10, within 10 days, you had a perfect fitting pair of jeans. Still, if the measurement was taken incorrectly in the first place or the sales staff was unfriendly, the added advantage of this technology would do little to build brand loyalty.

In order for technology to be most efficient, it's critical that it is user-friendly. On the front page of *The Age* newspaper (12 June 1991), a survey by the Australian National University claimed that Australians are often left more bewildered by the operation of some of the gadgets designed to make life easier!

> *While more than 60 percent of homes have videocassette recorders, 22 percent of people experience difficulty using them and 16 percent of people find it difficult to gain access to funds via automatic teller machines.*

And, I know it's not just Australians who get frustrated. Machinery should be truly user-friendly, as the benefits of using technology certainly outweigh the possible pitfalls. Technology is not a panacea for delivering service, but it can dramatically improve service delivery if used cleverly, in line with customer needs and expectations.

I was given a mug at a technology conference with a most amusing inscription:

> *Thank you for calling our customer service department.*
> *If you have a complaint, please press 1.*

If you would like an apology, please press 2.
If you would like an excuse, please press 3.
If you would like an extension of credit, please hang up immediately.
And, if you would like to send a mild electric shock to whoever
designed this system, please press 4.

What a humorous but serious message. I remembered another of my mother's maxims that "truer things are often said in jest."

Frankly, I'm happy not to be on the cutting edge of technology in case I get cut if I don't get it right. As technology is not the linchpin of my business, I'm happy to follow and learn from others, although I recognize I can't be too far behind.

Technology can certainly help. For more than 10 years now, I've ordered pizza for home delivery from a number stored in automatic dial on my telephone. As soon as the phone is answered, I am asked for my phone number. That is quickly keyed into a computer. The screen immediately displays my name, phone number, address, nearest cross street, and what was previously ordered. The pizza employee then asks if I'd like what I ordered last week and guarantees it will be delivered within 30 minutes or I receive a $3 refund.

They can also track whether or not the pizza was delivered on time, if I want a drink or dessert, and whether or not I've complained about service in the past. This data allows them to have more information on me so as to be responsive to my needs and desires.

Better still, when I call a taxi or courier, they don't even need my phone number as it is automatically displayed for their dispatcher. It saves me and them time and reduces errors.

A number of restaurants have introduced electronic order books for waiters and waitresses. It lists the daily specials and as soon as an order is taken, it is relayed immediately to the kitchen or bar so preparation can begin without delay. No more arguments about whose order came in first or possible errors due to illegible handwriting.

What used to be considered leading edge is now the norm, and most international hotels have personalized voice mail that results in callers leaving more messages. It is especially popular with foreign or multilingual guests who aren't as likely to receive accurate, detailed messages from family or business acquaintances back home because the hotel operators can't translate. But other companies have found voice mail a negative to customer service as customers complain about getting transferred from one message machine to another.

Voice mail can be useful technology, but can't appease an irate customer or make a follow-up sale. So, it is important to do thorough market research and perhaps make voice mail optional when people call. Don't let customers succumb to "death by voice mail"—which could be the death knell of your organization.

Most people like personalization without intruding on their privacy. I always remember my second visit to a hotel in Singapore when I was greeted with a friendly: "Welcome back to the Sheraton Towers Ms. DeVrye. It's a pleasure to see you again."

Very simply, they had that data on a single computer screen for the front desk clerk to readily access. A client told me that he was "blown away" when he went to the bar at the Oriental Hotel in Hong Kong, having previously stayed at the same hotel chain in Bangkok. As soon as he gave his room number, the bartender asked if he'd like his martini dry, as he had it in Thailand!

Technology can be particularly useful in large companies to give the impression of providing more personalized customer service. The secret is to have each customer feel they are being treated as an important customer, even though they may be only one of thousands of daily transactions.

4 Big isn't necessarily better—only better is better

Often larger organizations lose sight of individual customers as they lack personal interaction. Employees in small businesses usually understand more fully the implications of repeat business to the success of the organization.

For 18 years I'd been a loyal customer of one of Australia's oldest and biggest banks. One year I received notification that I could pick up my new credit card from their Melbourne branch. I'd lived in Sydney, hundreds of miles away, for the last eight years, and this was the third or fourth time I'd informed them I had changed branches.

I phoned the number listed on the letterhead. I was greeted by a cheery enough "Good Morning," but things deteriorated from there. I asked for the card to be delivered to my Sydney branch in the next day or two. The woman on the other end of the phone informed me it had nothing to do with her and I would have to call or fax the Melbourne branch. I explained I had done so on previous occasions and couldn't see why I should have to incur another expense for their error. She became rather annoyed and said: "It's got nothing to do with me."

I asked to speak to her supervisor, at which stage she hung up. I marched down to the branch and transferred all my accounts to a smaller bank around the corner.

The service from this smaller bank was incident-free for a number of months. I was then interested in buying an investment property and called to inquire about their loan policy. As it wasn't convenient to visit the bank, I simply gave them a statement of assets, liabilities, and income over the phone. I was only at the stage of looking and didn't need a firm commitment but an indication of what sort of loan was likely to enable me to take a look at the property market.

The woman was very courteous and said she would call me within the next 24 hours. True to her word, she called the next day and indicated a sum far greater than I expected. She explained how she had reached the calculations and said: "I hope you don't mind but I took the liberty of calling a couple of real estate agents in the area to determine the likely rental return and calculated the loan on that basis."

I'm now an absolutely delighted customer of the small bank, which differentiated itself not on price or product range, as after all the loans and interest rates are much the same, but on service.

"Perceived service leaders can charge 9-10 percent more for the same basic product"(Zemke and Schaaf 1989). This is so. Satisfied customers feel that delivery of goods and courteous service justify higher charges. Organizations disappear without customers. This should always be remembered before offering less than reasonable service. Service pays.

If large organizations could make every employee feel it's *their* business, service and profitability would inevitably increase.

5   Create a corporate culture dedicated to service excellence

Every employee should understand the significance of the question: "If my job ceased to exist, would the customer notice?"

The corollary is: "If there were no customers, I'd be out of a job. What then can I do to make myself invaluable to the customer and the boss?"

Leaders need to constantly communicate the vision for their organizations. The late Akio Morita, founder of Sony, didn't see his company in the electronics business. Certainly stereos and the famous Walkman are an integral part of the business, but he clearly had a vision of Sony being the leading entertainment company in the world, which is why they invested 3.5 billion dollars to buy Columbia Pictures. Employees of Sony are constantly reminded of the direction in which the organization is heading.

When the Road Traffic Authority in the state of Victoria in Australia expanded its vision for service delivery, a senior manager in their organization told me that their vision wasn't to fill potholes or install x number of traffic lights but "To build a better Victoria." They planned to do this not only through traditional road building, but by looking at alternative transportation to make Victoria a better place to live. This was no easy task for a government monopoly, but at least they made a start by articulating the big picture and putting internal service agreements in place to measure staff performance.

And it's a smart move if they can turn the theory into reality, realizing that many so-called monopolies no longer have the luxury of remaining a monopoly as many services can, and are being outsourced by the government. These aren't just the white-collar jobs of call centers or data processing, but even garbage pickup, groundskeeping, and security are no longer the sacred domain of the local council. Today, outside contractors and even more progressive municipal authorities offer more cost-effective solutions to taxpayers.

Again, it's not really within the scope of this book to comment extensively, but I personally believe it's important to also consider the human side of the equation. When an organization is outsourcing, loyal, long-term employees should not be dismissed for the sake of saving a few short-term dollars, without giving those affected an opportunity to lift their game and be more competitive.

Lord Colin Marshall, the man responsible for the dramatic improvement in British Airways service and market share, advocates that vision and cultural change must be directly driven by the chief executive officer. He constantly communicated the message that every employee must see the business as the customer really sees it, not how employees would like customers to see it. He claimed to spend not less than 25 percent of his time changing the culture. He attended customer service seminars and quality presentations to the front line, and often had a drink with them afterward to further reinforce the message in a more casual setting.

At one stage, one of my largest clients was American Express Corporate Travel, and I was most impressed by a regional vice president who had monthly meetings for groups of 30, rotating the more than 300 consultants. At those meetings he always gave up-to-date profitability figures—the good news and the bad. He had the team draw pictures of how they felt about the organization, which were plastered on the wall, and also had the room decorated with photos of their high achievers to celebrate their success. In addition, he had open forums where he encouraged frank questions from the relatively small group. As an attendee at these monthly meetings for four years, I witnessed that his team certainly didn't always agree with what he said, but idolized the ground he walked on. They felt they got a fair hearing, and he always shared the immediate challenges and reinforced the long-term vision with his inspiring words and great sense of humor.

Churches also have this challenge of leadership and how to best market their message. The Pentecostal minister of a congregation in Brisbane informed me his church had grown from 48 parishioners attending a little corner church to the redevelopment of a one-acre site with more than 1,100 "customers" attending regularly!

"We're in the business of marketing Jesus," he explained, "and our success really depends on how we package the product." He told me he introduced a customer satisfaction survey for parishioners to find out reasons why they did/didn't come to church and what they most liked or disliked about the service and environment. He asked: "What can I do better to make church a better experience for you?"

He discovered that he had a lot of time-sensitive professionals who wanted easy parking, so he made those arrangements.

The number-one reason a person didn't return after an initial visit was simply because they weren't asked. Now, within 24 hours of a first visit to the church, the potential new member is approached by a long-standing member of the church and made to feel welcome. As the minister explained: "The church is not the minister—it's the people."

Likewise, any business is not the boss—it's the customers.

6 The value of repeat business and frequency marketing

In any business, repeat business is the best. Chances are that you may not have heard of a wombat, let alone the WOMBAT theory. A wombat is a little furry Australian animal, not as well known as a kangaroo or koala. And, the WOMBAT theory simply stands for Word Of Mouth—Best Advertising Technique. You can have the most glossy magazine ads, wonderful commercials on TV or radio, but if two friends are talking and one is knocking your product and service, who will have the most credibility—the expensive advertising campaign or the friend? Certainly, advertising helps build brand awareness, but without actual delivery of the promise and happy customers who reinforce the advertising, you won't have them spread your brand awareness via word of mouth.

Frequency marketing is gaining increased popularity as a tool to identify and maintain loyal customers. It aims to reward and encourage existing customers by locking them in "golden cuff links." It first started with frequent flyer programs in airlines and soon extended to hotels.

Frequency of the use of services—be it flight, car leasing, driving, telephone calling, or regular buying from a commercial outlet—has led some organizations to reward such customers with discounts, club memberships, bonus goods, and newsletters. Satisfied customers are repeat customers and will tell others of the service they receive. They are a form of free advertising.

I've seen evidence that shows customers with frequent buyer points spend more money than those without, but surely there's still a limited pool of disposable income. However, with the increase in so-called loyalty programs, one can't help but wonder whether the term is a misnomer, as how can a customer be truly loyal if they're a member of all loyalty programs offered by airlines or retailers?

A speaker on technology, based in Queensland, offers a simple, interesting, and obviously effective use of the Internet for creating client loyalty. In his book, *Internetprofit.com.au*, Monte Huebsch outlines a case study of how a local retailer uses targeted e-mail to address potential customers with the word they like to hear most—their name.

■ C A S E   S T U D Y

The most important word to your customers and clients is their name. We do not believe in "spam" or e-mail that is not personalized and all our e-mails contain your name, usually in the subject header. This is a practice you should consider adopting.

While the media is usually covering the Web and its potential, it is worth remembering that a customer or client must go to a Web site. They must know its address and have the TIME to visit it.

E-mail is different. It is an active medium. Most people will at least check their e-mail once a day, while they may only "surf" the Internet once a week.

An e-mail that has a customer or client name in the subject will usually be looked at and read before it is discarded. Targeted and personalized e-mail is a MUST HAVE tool for any business that uses the Internet.

The following actual case study will make the point much clearer.

This case study relates to a retail store that sells electronic games. Given that the products were electronic, a foray onto the Internet was a natural progression since all its customers had some sort of electronic device, but how many had access to the Internet?

We started by placing a bowl in the store that people could leave their name and e-mail address in. Once a month, a drawing was held and the winner received a coupon for a gift certificate at the store. The "winner" was announced via e-mail, of course. People who placed their name and e-mail in the bowl also became members of the store's "Platinum" club.

This was NOT a newsletter but a loyalty program. The first mailing was personalized with the recipient's name and contained an offer to come to the store with a copy of the e-mail for 5 percent discount on any purchase. The recipient had to come in by the following Friday. Sales went UP!

The second e-mail announced an upcoming sale and invited the Platinum club members to come in early with a copy of their personalized e-mail so they could take advantage of the sales prices prior to the actual sale and before all the good games were taken. Again, sales went up.

The store owner was beginning to see the potential of the personalized e-mail program. What he wished to accomplish next were more members in his Platinum club. To this end he sent out another club announcement. This announcement had both the existing club member's first and last name and asked that the e-mail be printed out and distributed to the club member's family and friends for them to receive an introductory offer of 10 percent off anything in his store. It went further by announcing that any e-mails brought in with the club member's name on it would be kept and the club member would receive a lottery ticket for each referral when they next came into the store.

Sales went up and so did club membership, dramatically!

Since the personalized e-mails were sent from a database, the store owner decided to record customer purchases in the same database. This allowed him to target a specific subset of customers for new releases of game software that came out fitting their user profile. By this method he was increasing his customer service while upgrading and cross selling his clients. By using the same database, he could question customers about their desire to purchase a new or updated game and this helped him control his purchasing and inventory.

He had now successfully created a coupon program, a sale program, a referral program, and an inventory program.

What next?

Next, he added a "value" to each personalized e-mail. By the customer collecting store e-mails, they gained the shop's own frequent flyer type points in the club and were eligible for discounts after collecting a certain number of e-mails. This kept people reading and staying subscribed in his club. This was a great loyalty program as he slowly turned his e-mail into a sort of club "currency."

On last contact with his company, they were including gaming "cheats" in their personalized e-mails. This was both a service and a program of planned obsolescence, as once a client had mastered a particular game, they usually returned to buy another!

Please remember that his company lacked a Web site and was not selling anything via the Internet. The whole program was built around customer service and support. This type of program is an absolute must for any company that has a portion of their client base connected to the Internet. As more people become connected, this program will move from a luxury to a necessity.

—(Huebsch 1999)

Entire books are written on frequency marketing and vision, so suffice it to say that any leader needs to believe in a vision of superior service for his or her organization and constantly communicate that to all employees.

You don't necessarily need elaborate marketing plans to achieve this. "Mama," of Mama's Spaghetti House in the Sydney suburb of Neutral Bay, fully understands the significance of this concept. As we left one night a few years ago, after enjoying a lovely Italian meal, she came running after us to return our tip and share a home truth of the success of her restaurant, while others are closing down:

"No, no. It is me who must thank you for coming. Take this extra money back. I want you to come again."

And, we will!

And speaking of communication, please make sure you avoid sending communications such as the following, which was sent from a computer company:

We offer quality hardware and software products with some day customer service second to none.

There's a big difference between same day service and someday service! Also it's essential to encourage employees to share their views of the future. Traditionally, many are reluctant to do so, but everyone must work together to look toward tomorrow today, as there are no guarantees of a parking space for life on the superhighway of the future.

After 10 years at IBM, I probably shouldn't admit that I occasionally get frustrated with computers and on one such occasion, the person providing hardware and software support to my small business sent me the following e-mail, which I have no idea if it's true or not—but it made me chuckle at a time I didn't feel technology failure was any laughing matter.

PC Rage
54 percent of computer users recently surveyed have experienced PC rage—extreme reactions to system problems, including screaming, swearing, threatening, hitting, dropping, or throwing of computer equipment, as well as abusing others, attacking other objects, resigning from jobs, and self-mutilation. Apart from triggering frustration, the prevalence of computer problems such as program crashes, virus infections, and lack of disk space represents very real data and productivity issues for individuals and corporations.

He assured me that my frustrations were perfectly normal, which I suppose is the key reason I outsource that function in my operations, as I admittedly sometimes find it frightening how dependent I've become on technology in my business. And when I get really frustrated, he calmly replies: "Would you rather go back to a pencil and paper?" . . . to which, of course, I have no sensible retort.

SEVEN KEY POINTS
in this chapter on vision:

1   A long-term vision, combined with a solid action plan, will produce lasting results.

2   Know the average lifetime value of your customers.

3   Bigger isn't better—only better is better.

4   Combine the "high tech" and the "high touch" to use technology.

5   Constantly communicate your vision of service excellence so every employee feels like it's *their* business.

6   Repeat business is the most valuable.

7   In my own organization, I will improve service through vision by:

_____

_____

_____

_____

_____

_____

_____

- **S**ELF-ESTEEM

- **E**XCEED EXPECTATIONS

- **R**ECOVER

- **V**ISION

5 Improve

- **C**ARE

- **E**MPOWERMENT

If you're not getting better . . .
you're getting worse.

1   Continually improve or give the competition a chance to catch up

"Continuous improvement" may have been viewed as the buzz phrase about quality service in the 1990s, but firms that succeed well into the 21st century will have embraced the concept far more than by mere lip service. The thriving and surviving enterprises of the future will be relentless in their quest to continually look at ways to improve their customer service levels.

They will recognize that no matter how successful they may have been in the past, there is no guarantee of future prosperity. There is no room for complacency among the service leaders of today.

"Service Darwinism" is the name of the game for those organizations that constantly evolve with the marketplace, to exceed the expectations of their customers. However, not just survival of the fittest, but survival of the fastest and the smartest . . . will be the catch phrase for those organizations that maintain longevity.

This point is illustrated in comments by leading American business authors on changes within IBM, my former employer. In 1981, when Tom Peters first published his best-seller, *In Search of Excellence*, he applauded IBM as an excellent service leader by commenting: "IBM really cares about service."

Six years later, in 1987, he was less complimentary in another book, *Thriving on Chaos*. In that he states: "IBM's service has become a bit tattered in recent years."

Two years later, in 1989, Ron Zemke and Dick Schaaf wrote in *The Service Edge*: "IBM wrote the book on customer service . . . and threw it away. And, what's more . . . the competition has written chapters of their own."

In that time, the IBM share price lost more than 50 percent of its market value. However, under new leadership, IBM has taken significant steps since 1989 to return to the basic principle of providing the best customer service. I believe IBM is still a great company, but it became somewhat arrogant during the 1980s and believed in its own success to the detriment of the service objective. For a period of years, many IBM employees lost sight of user needs, as they strove to impress the marketplace with the latest technology.

At the time of writing, IBM stocks, with splits, were near an all-time record high and I'm still proud to have worked for them and equally pleased that I kept my stock! There are no guarantees they, or any other information technology company, will continue to prosper in the rapidly changing industry, but they certainly took significant steps to regain customer confidence and to make the company less top heavy and more customer-focused. Continuation of such action, plus always keeping an open mind to innovation—recognizing that they are no longer the only "kid on the computer block"—should reap dividends for shareholders in the future. I believe the company nicknamed "Big Blue" now fully recognizes that "Bigger isn't better."

Only better is better! If you're not constantly striving to improve, you simply give the competition a chance to catch up.

I love the comment in Bill Gates's book *Business At The Speed of Thought*, where the founder of Microsoft says:

In three years, every product in my company will be obsolete. The only question is whether we'll make them obsolete or somebody else will.

I personally believe there is incredible optimism in such comments, but again, we need to be cautious and not blindly believe Bill Gates or anybody else who says they have all the answers to what's happening with the speed of technology. Just as couriers made inroads into the postal market, so too the Internet will have an impact upon couriers. But don't abandon your postal or courier service without first thinking through as many implications as possible. After all, *you're* most likely to be the person with the answers to many of the questions in your business.

And, if you try some new whiz-bang technology and it doesn't work out, never be too proud to revisit an "old-fashioned" or different way of doing things as technology, in itself, isn't always the instant fix some people would have you believe.

For example, I recently heard a presentation by the marketing director of a large, multinational pharmaceutical company who provided colorful Microsoft Powerpoint graphic illustrations of how they had introduced a sophisticated voice recognition system as part of their customer inquiry strategy. He was able to clearly quantify that it had improved turnaround time and reduced staffing costs. This all sounded impressive and many in the audience were frantically taking copious notes when he then shifted his emphasis and stunned everyone by outlining why they had abandoned this expensive technology in less than a year.

> *Certainly, our turnaround was faster and our costs lower, but we also had lower rates of customer satisfaction, which we could eventually see contributing to lower profits. So we hired retired nurses as we found our patients had a much higher level of trust with a "real life" compassionate voice on the other end of the phone. The nurses still had access to all the intelligent data on the system, but sick and worried people really needed the reassurance of a human voice when they had an inquiry about a pharmaceutical product. Sure, our staffing costs went up, but it was worth every cent in terms of happier customers and longer-term dividends.*

I was suitably impressed by this man's candid admission of his mistake in the rush to introduce new technology. Possibly they could have avoided a costly capital investment if they had completely thought through the repercussions earlier, rather than rush headlong down the technology path, as many are tempted to do to show they're "with it," "leading edge," or whatever. But, how more costly, if stubbornness or ego had prevented this marketing leader from recognizing his error early on. Don't get me wrong—I believe technology can assist greatly in customer service, as outlined in the previous chapter. However, we also need to look at continual improvement not simply as being more technology, but better systems—whether they be technological or human in nature.

2   Change . . . or else!

Extremely successful corporations often find change most difficult. In 1975, Wrigley had more than 90 percent of the chewing-gum market, when the competition introduced sugarless gum (Fortune, August 1990). At that stage, the newest of the Wrigley's product line brands had been introduced in 1914! By the late 1970s, their market share had declined to 33 percent!

Corporations need to heed the writing on the wall—change, or else!

Change for the sake of change would be ludicrous. The key factor is to look constantly at customer needs and expectations in order to be fully responsive to changes that occur in the marketplace.

The older the organization, the harder it may be to change or adapt. Past success gives no guarantee of similar success in the future.

Some organizations move out of less profitable goods to areas where they have to learn the rules all over again. However, if there is a commitment and a willingness to learn, these organizations can be winners.

Joban Kosan is a multidimensional company that shifted its emphasis from coal to leisure resorts. When they won the highly coveted Deming Quality award, the managing director accepted the award and said: "This is like qualifying for university. Now, we need to start and work even harder."

That's the mark of service leaders in this century. They are never completely satisfied with their progress. They will be relentless in their quest for continuous improvement and never take their own press, no matter how successful, too seriously.

3 All employees need to look for better ways

Overnight changes and immediate results do not happen. You need to set short-, medium-, and long-term plans—and start today.

There will be many reasons for not improving or changing. Have you ever heard: "I've been here 25 years and we've never done it that way; and survived quite nicely, thank you." Or, worse still: "I've been here 25 years and we tried it that way . . . once."

Remember that the six most expensive words in business are:
We've always done it that way.

Plan now for continuous improvement. In that planning process, it's critical to first analyze and improve on areas that customers really care about.

To invest considerable time and money to reduce the waiting time in lines from five minutes to three is folly. Only after a vast expenditure of money and staff hours did one bank discover that their customers could not differentiate between a five-minute and a three-minute wait. The customers would have preferred resources to have been spent on extended hours of operation for their convenience.

Don't provide improvements that you *think* customers want. Make sure first to find out what those wants are. Involve all employees in the planning process for continual improvement of customer satisfaction.

Jan Carlzon recognized the importance of this. As chief executive officer of Scandinavian Airlines in the mid-1980s he turned the organization around from an $18 million loss to a $54 million profit in 18 months by focusing on improving the "little things."

When he was first appointed as chief executive officer, he called all employees together in an aircraft hangar and frankly explained the financial difficulties facing the airline. He admitted he didn't have all the answers. He told them he needed their help if the airline was to survive. Not everyone had face-to-face contact with customers, but in a customer-service organization each is working in a chain, which ultimately serves someone. Efficiency, accountability, and courtesy should be present in every sphere of that service.

Carlzon proceeded to inform all employees that if they weren't serving a customer, they should be serving someone who was!

4 Little things make a big difference— "moments of truth"

Jan Carlzon also outlined a concept that he named "moments of truth." This was defined as any encounter between a member of the airline and the public that lasted more than 15 seconds. It was a moment of truth when a customer booked a ticket; when they checked their bag; when they were served a cup of coffee; and so on.

In the mid-1980s, market research indicated that if Scandinavian Airlines could improve their scheduling, they would gain market share. Carlzon certainly wanted to focus on this, but realized there were factors in scheduling, such as weather and air traffic control, that were outside the control of the airline. So he asked employees not only to focus on the major issue of more timely arrivals and departures, which he personally monitored, but also to pay attention to the little "moments of truth." It seemed too daunting to even try to improve departure times 100 percent but relatively easy to improve 100 individual moments of truth by 1 percent, for the same net impact on overall improvement.

In Scandinavian Airlines, they amazingly identified more than 10 million moments of truth in a year. Carlzon challenged his employees to focus on improving each of those moments of truth by a small percentage. Collectively, this made an enormous difference to service levels in the airline. Twenty years later the airline is still profitable, but will they be in the future? Will you? The question is never how good you are . . . but are you good enough to want to get better? If, like Scandinavian Airlines, you can identify millions, or even just hundreds, of moments of truth and improve each one of them a tiny percentage point, imagine the overall improvement to your business.

What are the moments of truth in your organization?

- A customer can't get through on the phone.
- A customer can't find a parking spot.
- A customer is treated gruffly by an employee having a bad day.
- A customer continually receives errors in her accounts.

These are just a few examples of moments of truth. But moments of truth can be positive, as well as negative.

- A customer gets a shopping cart in a supermarket with four wheels that work—that is a positive moment of truth.
- The aisles are clear of debris—that is a moment of truth.
- Goods that customers want are stocked and attractively displayed—that is a moment of truth.
- The person at the checkout is friendly and efficient—that is a moment of truth.
- Customers' bags are properly packed, separating frozen produce from soap—that is a moment of truth.
- The bag does not break before the customer gets home—that is another moment of truth.

Think of *one* little thing you can do *today* to improve a moment of truth in your organization; and encourage each employee to do likewise.

Have you ever been ignored by a salesperson in a retail shop when you desperately wanted help? And pestered by them when you didn't? A number of years ago I walked into a computer retail store to inquire about a new PC. The young man had on a wrinkled shirt, a two-day beard growth, and body odor, so I left as soon as possible. Even though he may have been extremely technically capable, those moments of truth were too much for me to bear and I figured that if he couldn't use low-tech equipment, like a shower, razor, and iron, then he probably couldn't use more sophisticated computer equipment. Now, I know that was irrational on my part, but the downfalls in his moments of truth caused me to leave before ever finding out the truth about his product knowledge!

Back to another example from another airline and this time with a concept worth emphasizing about improvement. Remember we spoke in Chapter 2 about expectations and the difference between adding value and cost; using an example of a tablecloth at a fast food restaurant. In the competitive airline industry, Delta Air had asked all employees for suggestions. One young man, working in the garbage department for only a few weeks, noticed as he emptied the food trays into big plastic garbage bags, that many of the passengers hadn't eaten their lettuce or parsley garnish, so he suggested that they eliminate that garnish as a way of avoiding waste. We can imagine that the hierarchy's first reaction might have been: "But, we've always had the lettuce" and they certainly didn't envisage it would save a great deal of money. However, desperate for any cost savings whatsoever, they implemented this young man's suggestion. He hadn't been bound by the parameters that they'd always done it that way—and much to management's surprise, they didn't simply save a few hundred dollars but more than 1.5 million a year. Because, even though the young man hadn't articulated it as such, the lettuce was adding cost to the airline—not value to the majority of the passengers. Cost or value? Cost or value? Keep asking that question whenever you're talking about continuous improvement and ask again and again . . . what is the equivalent of the lettuce in my organization?

5 Invest in training people for service excellence

No chapter on improvement would be complete without some mention of training to provide employees with the tools and motivation to focus on continuous improvement.

As stated earlier, it is important to hire positive people in the first place. No amount of training will turn a person with a negative attitude into a service superstar. Hire people who want to learn and are curious to discover better ways of doing things.

Hire people willing to invest in themselves and who view education as a lifelong pursuit. They want to learn, not simply because their employer forces them to, but because it helps them to help others. This ultimately helps them to help themselves and improve themselves and their lifestyles.

Don't adopt training for the sake of training. Any worthwhile training program should have clearly stated objectives and work-related outcomes. Don't spend a cent until you have checked the references of the trainer, consultant, or speaker.

Employees should know that management supports the benefits of training and they aren't simply putting on an employee program because they have to spend the money.

It is strongly recommended that any service training start at the top. That is not to say an executive should necessarily cover the same content as a front-line employee. But, if employees know that management places importance on training and invest their own time, they are more likely to take the training seriously.

Some form of service quality orientation should be compulsory for everyone in the organization and the chief executive officer shouldn't tolerate any of the management team saying: "I'm too busy."

Such messages signal that management isn't really committed to service improvement. It's easy for staff to see through a "Do as I say . . . not as I do" approach to training.

One of my largest clients is an international household name and I've spoken to the client's various team members every month for the last four years. The vice president of that division never ceases to amaze me by sitting through each of my presentations and introducing each session by saying: "I know some of you have heard this before. I've heard it more than any of you but I always hear something new or something I hadn't heard before, or need to be reminded of." He's an outstanding leader and I've probably learned as much as I've taught from his personal example over the years.

Some companies have long-standing training programs, whereas in other organizations, training is a new concept. If employees haven't participated before, they may be somewhat suspicious of attending. Those who haven't had a good experience at school may see training as uncomfortable, equating it with disciplinary measures in their educational past or an implication that they're not good at their jobs. To overcome any such apprehension, management needs to clearly outline the purpose and benefits of training in a non-threatening way.

Encourage staff to want to learn continually. Sending them on a training program, itself, isn't going to produce overnight results. Training needs to be aligned to other activities in the organization and constantly reinforced.

People are the most valuable asset in an organization. A company may invest money in bricks and mortar. Training is also an investment, not an expense. All the marble in the foyer and plush towels in a hotel room become insignificant if the staff are rude to customers.

Word-of-mouth advertising from satisfied customers who have experienced excellent service from your well-trained staff is far more convincing than paid advertising.

> *Hibernia Bank in the United States spends twice the industry average on training. The reward is that the bank receives in revenue about $100,000 per employee more than the industry average!*
> *Service standards at Hibernia state that tellers must greet customers at least once by name. Phones must be answered by the third ring and customers holding in line must be given a response in 20 seconds. Ironically, it doesn't take more people but about 5 percent fewer. Tom Van Berkam, senior vice president of human resources explains:*
> *"By providing better service, we can make fewer mistakes and people don't hang up in disgust and then call back, which means fewer and shorter incoming calls."*
> —On Achieving Excellence, newsletter by Tom Peters

Educating employees as to the importance of service is vital, regardless of the size of an organization. Tom O'Toole, the owner of an outstandingly successful bakery, Beechworth, in a small country town in Australia is often asked how he can afford to train his staff.

"What if you train 'em and they leave?" ask other small business owners in the town."

"Yeah," replies Tom dryly, "but what if I don't train 'em and they stay!"

6 Maintain the momentum

Most companies that start a service quality program eventually lose some momentum. The excitement and energy from the initial phases of the service training effort die down.

The challenge for managers is to maintain the momentum and continually keep people focused. Be sure to constantly reinforce consistent messages, so employees don't see service training as a passing fad.

If you're the boss, remember these two quotes:

1. If you refuse to accept anything but the best, you very often get it.

—Somerset Maugham

2. I am easily satisfied with the best.

—Winston Churchill

Continuous improvement for the delivery of quality service is not easy. But it is essential.

When looking at your organization you could think the task is too big. But, you must start somewhere. Break the task into manageable portions. Improvement of service quality won't happen overnight. However, everyone in the organization must start to do some little thing to improve a moment of truth . . . today!

SEVEN KEY POINTS
in this chapter on improvement:

1 No matter how good you are, if you're not getting better, you're getting worse.

2 Be responsive to change . . . .or else!

3 It's easier to improve 100 processes by 1 percent than a single process by 100 percent.

4 Continuous improvement starts at the top. No one is too senior to learn.

5 Encourage all employees to always look for a better way of doing things.

6 Maintain the momentum and focus every day on little things.

7 In my own organization, I will improve service through continuous improvement by:

_____

_____

_____

_____

_____

_____

_____

■ S ELF–ESTEEM

■ E XCEED EXPECTATIONS

■ R ECOVER

■ V ISION

■ I MPROVE

6 Care

■ E MPOWERMENT

*People don't care how much
you know until they know
how much you care.*

1   Customer-friendly systems—make it easy to do business with you

You never win an argument with a customer.

It's critical to genuinely care about each and every customer. In large organizations, which receive hundreds or thousands of calls or orders per day, it's tempting to think of customers as statistics, rather than focus on the fact that each of them has individual needs and differences.

In his best-selling book, *Reinventing Australia*, social researcher Hugh Mackay states an observation equally true in North America:

> *Australians are expressing a sharply increasing demand for improved quality of customer service and that demand generally focuses on the need for more attention to be paid to the personal relationship between customer and service provider. Again, the underlying need for human contact emerges: "treat me as if I belong here; acknowledge me as a person; let's act as if this commercial relationship is a personal relationship."*

> —(Mackay 1993)

A woman once came up to me after one of my presentations and commented that she had adopted children and always tried to make her customers feel as if she had adopted them as well. As I was an adopted child myself, her comparison moved me deeply and links to the best definition that I've ever heard of adoption—attributed to a four-year-old girl telling her classmates: "Adoption is when you move from the tummy of one mummy into the heart of another."

I was initially somewhat surprised with the analogy to customers, and a little lost for words at the time the comment was made, but on reflection I thought it was a lovely sentiment to try and make customers feel as if you'd adopted them because true customer care comes from the heart.

Each of us is a customer regularly and we appreciate that customer care does not equate to some insincerely muttered phrase such as: "Have a nice day."

Customers expect service. They don't really care about your problems or any strategic plans management may have in place to fix them. They only care about how they are treated at a particular time.

They're not concerned about the hardworking people behind the scenes . . . or budget restraints . . . or staff cutbacks. There may be legitimate reasons why their problem has occurred, but customers don't want to know. They pay *you* to worry about *their* problems. Nothing is ever gained by winning an argument and losing a customer! If you want customers, treat them well because . . .

It costs five times more
to obtain a new customer
than to retain an existing one.
    —(TARP data; Technical Assistance Research Program for U.S. Department of
                                                                    Consumer Affairs)

Everyone in an organization is responsible for customer service, not only the sales representative or the telephone operator. People working behind the scenes in accounts and delivery are also responsible.

All aspects of service need to be customer-focused because it costs five times more to obtain a new customer than it does to retain an existing one. So, again, remember that you want them to "boomerang back" and everyone in the organization needs to play their part by keeping existing customers satisfied.

Caring about customers means making your organization "user-friendly." This term does not relate to computer hardware or software but simply to making it easy for customers to do business with you.

- Can they get through on your telephones?
- Are they always greeted courteously?
- Can they find a parking spot?
- Are your accounts easy to understand?
- Do you deliver?
- Are you open at times convenient to them?

These are the services you expect. Treat customers as you would like to be treated. Put yourself in their shoes to see if your organization is truly customer-friendly.

A Californian bank, operating primarily in a retirement community, applies this brilliantly. As part of their training program for young tellers, they wear glasses smeared with Vaseline, put cotton wool in their ears, and tape their fingers together. This allows the service providers to experience firsthand some of the challenges of aging and more fully appreciate that many of their customers may be partially blind, deaf, or arthritic. By truly putting themselves in the customer's shoes, the teenage tellers implemented more user-friendly suggestions for the elderly customers, such as larger print on checkbooks and pens with thicker grips.

Chairs and desks and magnifying glasses were not expensive to provide. But many banking institutions have a long way to go to provide services appropriate to elderly customers' needs . . . actually to improve services for all ages, as many progressive financial institutions are now doing.

Some organizations—British Gas, for example—provide telephone information services for aged people or those that are physically impaired. Full telephone advice is available on appliances, and inquiries are recorded on customers' files.

I can't recall where I read that one branch office of H&R Block improved their bottom line dramatically by providing a better service to one hearing-impaired customer. One of their administrators had processed income tax forms for a deaf client for a few years and any questions were handled by passing notes back and forth across the desk. The employee decided to learn sign language to better serve this customer and they now have a huge client base of other hearing-impaired persons. That's truly listening to a customer in a unique way!

One of the biggest improvements to service levels in Australia in recent times has been the introduction of weekend and evening business hours. Convenient hours for busy customers were long overdue so supermarkets are now open at times outside normal working hours.

I was delighted when my local supermarket first opened in the evenings. I was on my way to the nearby neighborhood shop, for emergency supplies of dog food and milk, when I noticed the local Woolworth's was open until midnight. I learned it was for a three-month trial to determine whether there was customer demand in the area. As a matter of principle, I stockpiled on dog food, soap, and a whole variety of nonperishable items. It was a delight to push my shopping cart down uncrowded aisles. I knew management would be monitoring sales after 9 p.m., so I wanted to help boost their totals. I wasn't spending more money than I normally would, but was doing so in one hit. Thousands of other customers also welcomed more convenient hours and the three-month pilot scheme has now become a permanent fixture.

My only complaint, in relation to customer-friendly supermarket shopping, is that I still can't understand why we have the sophisticated technology to be able to put satellites in outer space but still can't invent a shopping cart with four smoothly turning wheels!

But to that comment, a friend only replies . . . "Order online!"

A store should be truly user-friendly. Goods should be displayed clearly and be easy to reach. Many organizations are not open at times when people can more easily patronize them.

Supermarkets and hardware stores aren't the only ones opening on weekends to be more user-friendly. Realtors, hairdressers, and a number of other services are now becoming more readily available at weekends.

Tradespeople could certainly learn from these service examples. They should make firm, time-tabled bookings, give quotes, and do the job. Some do, but many still say they are unable to guarantee a set time and price. Hopefully all small businesses will recognize that guaranteeing accurate arrival times, or even giving a one-hour time range to allow for traffic, will give them a competitive edge.

With the proliferation of cell phones, there is absolutely no excuse for not letting the customer know if unexpected delays occur. Most customers will tolerate, often begrudgingly, that you're late if a valid reason is given but they will no longer tolerate what used to be the norm—continually being kept waiting with no communication as to the reason for the delay.

On a visit to a specialist doctor recently, I was mildly annoyed when I was kept waiting more than half an hour for my first appointment. But I know that's the norm for most doctors and understand that they can't always accurately predict the amount of time it may take to diagnose a patient, so I was prepared with my own reading material (as I certainly don't want to waste my time reading the array of outdated magazines in most waiting rooms!).

On the second visit I was kept waiting an hour and if I hadn't been committed to treatment with this specialist, I would have left. On the way out I commented to the receptionist that I understood they may have delays but as I had to drive a number of miles to visit the doctor, I'd appreciate it if she could please call and let me know if they were running late so I could continue with productive work. I arrived for the third visit, confident there would be little delay, as I hadn't heard. An hour and a half later I was furious, as were other people in the waiting room. "Oh, he's always late and it really annoys us but there's not much we can do," everyone whispered out of earshot of the receptionist. My comments to her were not out of hearing range and I calmly but firmly expressed my dissatisfaction and said everyone else felt the same but we've been conditioned to be too intimidated by the professional status of doctors to say anything. She shrugged her shoulders and said that I should tell the doctor himself, which I duly did—after he'd finished his diagnosis. I also informed him that I spoke on behalf of the other people in the waiting room and that although we could appreciate emergencies, we certainly couldn't appreciate the practice of overbooking. This was obvious as during the course of conversation with other patients, we discovered that some of us had appointments within five minutes of each other when there was no way that a consultation could take such little time. I also informed him that I thought he was a brilliant specialist and worth every cent of the money I had spent from a medical standpoint, but outlined that my time was also valuable and that if I was kept waiting again, I'd be sending him an invoice for my hourly fee. After the initial shock, he put a note on the file and I've never been kept waiting since. But, I'm not sure about others.

Another example was during an air-traffic controllers' strike in Australia, which resulted in delays of all our major airlines. Most passengers appreciated that the delays were outside the control of the actual airline but one airline cleverly turned the "problem" into an opportunity by calling their frequent fliers as soon as they knew there would be a likely delay on their scheduled flight. They then gave those passengers the choice of coming to the airport and taking a chance on their original flight or rescheduling, whereas the other airlines made no attempt whatsoever to notify passengers and simply placed any blame for delays on the unions. None of the airlines had control over the delays, but one airline took control of the circumstances. That company created greater frequent flier loyalty by going that little extra distance by keeping customers in the information loop; and I, for one, became more brand loyal to them.

Mail-order shopping has been a part of Australian and American marketing history. The arrival of a department store catalog at rural

properties has been and still is a time for wishing and making decisions. Tape measures come out, budgets are examined, and order
forms filled in. This form of buying from catalogs proves that if an
organization delivers the goods of quality and provides personalized
service, it will have generations of satisfied customers.

There has been a great growth in this form of marketing since the
1950s. For people averse to shopping, it is an answer to their needs.
Alternative colors and styles are sent for the customer to have a
choice. Those not bought are returned. The providers are fulfilling
customers' needs.

Catalog and online shopping are becoming increasingly popular
among working families who prefer to shop from the comfort of their
home, regardless of what hours a shop may be open. One of the most
talked-about catalog businesses in the United States is L.L. Bean. They
offer a top quality range of products and give guaranteed delivery
dates. Their recent catalog stated that if you ordered before 5 p.m. on
December 22, they would guarantee delivery on Christmas Eve anywhere in the United States. You can place an order 24 hours a day on
a toll-free number. Friendly receptionists provide guidance on how to
take accurate measurements for clothing and suggest matching coordinates. I know a number of people, living in various parts of the
globe, who shop with them.

Another acquaintance told me how much he hated shopping. He
pointed to the wool jacket he wore and proudly announced he'd
bought it from an Amway catalog. Apparently, that particular jacket
was available in three different colors and only one was displayed in
the catalog. He wasn't sure which one to choose, nor was he sure of
his exact measurements. "No problem," said the order entry clerk.
"We'll send you all three colors in different sizes and you can keep
which one fits and return the rest."

The customer was delighted with the quality of the product and
also the service. It was truly making it easy for him to do business with
Amway; which is probably one explanation why catalog sales have
grown and are projected to increase even more significantly in
volume in the next decade.

This does not endorse Amway or L.L. Bean or any other company
with catalog or "e-tail" outlets, but simply provides illustrations of
how some companies make it easy for customers to do business with
them.

Not all organizations do so. A young travel consultant tried to sell an older client a particular tour package to London. He extolled the added benefits of the free nightlife tours but didn't appreciate that these were of little interest to the elderly client.

As part of retailing research, a female executive spent three years dressing and acting like an 85-year-old woman to learn how products and services work for the elderly (Zemke and Schaaf 1989). She found few things designed with senior citizens in mind. A salesperson in a pharmacy was most helpful to her when she was an attractive, 26-year-old New Yorker. But he stayed behind the counter and snarled when she was dressed in her meek, old-woman costume. From being a valued customer she became a nuisance, just because of her appearance—even though her purchase was exactly the same!

That's hardly caring about customers!

Rental car companies have a lot to learn about being user-friendly. The radio is inevitably programmed to nothing but loud rock stations, and I'm sure that's not the preference of the majority of drivers who would be middle-aged, middle-class patrons. But the young kids cleaning the car don't seem to realize this, and management doesn't seem to tell them. And I can't understand why I must pay about 50 percent more for gas if I don't fill up myself when returning the car. I'm usually running late for a plane and it would be so much easier if they charged me the going rate, plus a small premium to make it easier for me.

I hired a car at Melbourne airport and remembered to ask for a detailed street map. It amazes me that these are not standard issue in rental cars, where the majority of users are unfamiliar with the city in which they hire the car. (However, they will soon be unnecessary when satellite navigation becomes a standard feature.)

I had a fairly tight schedule and was frustrated to discover, as I was driving to my destination, the particular page I required had been torn from the book of maps. A few days later, when returning the car I mentioned the missing page to the clerk. I wasn't upset and only mentioned it so they could replace the page, to avoid another customer having the same problem. Rather than thank me and show empathy with my plight, she bluntly informed me that street maps were nothing more than a nuisance as you couldn't trust customers, who stole them or tore them and then added: "It's no use telling me about it as quite frankly, we're trying to phase them out."

Little did she realize that it was her job that would be phased out if other customers, like me, chose another company in future. And as someone who is "directionally challenged" at the best of times, I certainly don't need the added stress of an inaccurate or missing map!

Now let me tell you why I became brand loyal to another car rental company. My home had been burglarized just before a trip and I arrived at my destination realizing that I hadn't yet had time to replace my driver's license. The young assistant was able to determine that I'd rented with them before and, after signing a waiver, I was on my way.

Make it easy for your customers to do business with you, whatever your product may be.

It's frustrating when you come across a clerk who is more interested in filling out the forms than in treating you like a human being.

It's frustrating when the doors are opened after opening time and closed a few minutes before closing time. User-friendly organizations would open a few minutes ahead of the published time and close a few minutes after.

Just Jeans is a good example of a user-friendly retailer. They have a no-questions-asked refund policy and provide free, in-store alterations. You also leave the store with crisply pressed pants and a friendly smile from the salesperson! This is no coincidence. They have a two-day sales course for all new employees, not just on the products and techniques of using the cash register, but to ensure employees all understand the corporate philosophy that the customer is key to a successful operation.

2 Quality—near enough is not good enough!

Customer-friendly organizations care about quality in all aspects of their operations. They recognize that the customer appreciates the quality long after they have forgotten the price.

Quality is not an act. It is a habit.

—Aristotle

Quality is a habit . . . a way of life for service-focused organizations. They don't subscribe to the notion that "near enough is good enough." To quality-focused companies, 99 percent error-free is not good enough. If the airline industry in Australia were satisfied with a 99 percent error-free record, there would be 211 fatal crashes per day in Australia (Civil Aviation Authority)! Thankfully, pilots have the right to refuse to fly a plane. Each pilot inspects the plane before takeoff and if there is any question whatsoever about safety, the plane simply won't go.

Defect-free

"Six sigma" quality is the standard for which progressive organizations aim. It involves a complicated set of statistical analysis but, in simple terms, means that for any product or transaction there should be no more than 3.4 errors per million in any aspect of an organization's operation. That is, only 3.4 faulty products per million, or 3.4 inaccurate invoices per million, or 3.4 telephone calls that aren't responded to immediately. Six sigma is substantially more impressive than 99 percent error-free.

Six-sigma quality recognizes that there is a significant cost to bad service. Do it right the first time to reduce avoidable errors. Every cent you spend on doing things wrong or redoing them goes directly to the bottom line. It costs you money, or costs a customer money.

Every error adds to the cost of service, whether it be time (personnel and computer time) or extra phone lines to handle complaints. In addition, more satisfied customers talking to their friends and colleagues reduces your advertising costs.

Too often you hear excuses such as "But, I didn't have time to do it properly" and you can only ask why it is that they have the time to do the rework but not the time to do it right in the first place, which would have taken less time in the long run!

In terms of caring . . . be care-ful . . . not care-less!

If each person in your organization is care-ful and passes on defect-free work to the next person, the end product will be defect-free.

A defect is not just a faulty part or failed component. A defect is anything that causes a customer to be less than delighted. It could be an error in an account, slow delivery of a service, or inconsiderate treatment.

In Australia, 99 percent defect-free would approximately translate into:

- over 1 million faulty drug prescriptions every year (based on figures provided from NHS Renumeration Per Prescription Data and 1991-92 Health Insurance Commission Annual Report.);
- 10,701 lost mail items per day.

And, since the United States has a population more than 10 times that of Australia, you can multiply those figures to get an estimate. Looking at simple, everyday transactions like that, it's easy to appreciate that 99 percent isn't good enough.

Would you be satisfied if your electricity and telephone worked 99 percent of the time? If your car started 99 times out of 100? By asking these basic questions, it's easy to see that 99 percent error-free operations within your own business are equally unacceptable!

There has been increasing recognition that quality is critical to our economic survival. Quality is openly talked about in boardrooms and on factory floors. It's mentioned in just about every major company's annual report. An annual report of a major Australian building company emphasized the company's commitment by having this phrase emblazoned on the front cover:

(Company X) is committed to building in quality by providing customers with innovative products and services that fully satisfy their needs.

Unfortunately, they only paid lip service to the slogan of quality service and are struggling today.

The Australian Quality Awards, sponsored by the Australian Quality Council, are similar to the prestigious Baldrige Awards in the United States. They recognize outstanding efforts by companies striving for quality results. The Baldrige Awards are a coveted sort of Academy Awards of the American business world—and it's important to celebrate the success of quality focused companies in order to remain globally competitive.

Each year gala dinners are held to recognize those large, medium-sized, and smaller organizations, in both the private and public sectors, that were able to demonstrate, by international comparison, that they are achieving world competitive performance levels.

Quality does not automatically equate with expense and prestige. Quality also means to work smarter, to maximize available resources. An excellent example was given by the executive chef of an Australian airline. When he was first appointed, he visited various locations around the country to inspect food quality and solicit information from local staff on recommended ways to make improvements. He discovered that menus were all set in Melbourne and, although excellent, it was far from cost-efficient. Head office dictated every location would have a set gourmet meal in first class. That meant Tasmanian salmon had to be air freighted more than a thousand miles to Darwin and strawberries to Alice Springs, whereas barramundi was readily abundant in those locations and could be an equal taste sensation at a fraction of the cost, without the worry of transport. The end result was less frustrated local employees and higher quality food at less than half the price to the airline. Now, that's a quality result! Quality has become the accepted language of international business, but it's not enough to be fluent in the language. Companies that are prospering not only talk quality—they deliver it continually!

■ CASE STUDY

How to Tackle My Quality Problems . . . and Why Should I?
by Liz Burrows, MBA Quality Assurance Manager, Blackmores Vitamins

Quality in the manufacturing industry can be measured in hard numbers: "Defect levels in parts produced by Machine X have been reduced by 5.6 percent," "Yields are now running at 97 percent, an improvement over the last year's 95.5 percent."

Both statements give you a quantitative idea of the improvement in the quality of your product (or, on the downside, can show how bad you are becoming). To get these statements, data is gathered and manipulated in such a way that you know where you stand, and later, after you have made improvements, how much better you are.

How can you get such hard facts to measure a frequent intangible like "quality of customer service"? After all, if you can measure it, surely you can measure an improvement, which is what you should be striving for. The good news is that this gathering and manipulation of data can be applied to such an intangible. The technique uses statistics, which is a word misunderstood, feared and, unfortunately, often ignored when related to anything other than the manufacturing environment.

Certainly you might know that you have a greater share of the market than your customers—statistics are already applied to the service industry to tell you that much. But wouldn't you rather know why, and what areas you can still improve on?

Within the manufacturing industry, the use of quality tools in problem solving is widespread, not just because they get results, but because of their simplicity. Industry has found that these tools are most powerful when placed in the hands of the workers, and these are often people with a basic education who fear the application of mathematics to anything other than the cost of lunch.

The seven common quality tools are:

- Pareto diagram
- Control chart
- Graph
- Histogram
- Tally-sheet
- Cause-and-effect diagram
- Scatter diagram

More about Pareto diagrams and the other quality tools can be found in *Mastering the Tools of QC*, by Hajime Karatsu and Toyoki Ikeda. As this book focuses on service, this section will deal with only one, the Pareto diagram, as it is the most useful tool for answering:

- Where are my problems?
- Which problems should I tackle first?
- How do I know if I have improved?

The Pareto diagram was named after an Italian economist, and gave rise to the Pareto principle. This is often known as the 80-20 rule, as you usually find that 80 percent of your problems come from 20 percent of causes. In other words, if you have identified 25 causes, or reasons for customer dissatisfaction, you will find that 80 percent of your dissatisfaction is due to only five (20 percent of 20) causes. This will automatically tell you that if you minimize these top five causes, your customer service problems will be reduced dramatically. One look at a Pareto diagram will show you that no matter how many of the trivial few causes you eliminate, it will not make very much difference to the end results at all— customer satisfaction.

A typical Pareto diagram is shown below. One important point in constructing a Pareto diagram is to plot causes rather than phenomena. For example, instead of putting "Goods arrived, water

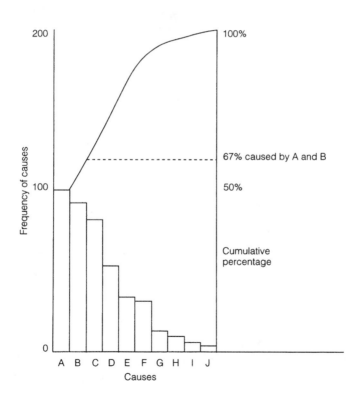

damage," determine how many times it occurred due to a leaking covered truck, or whether the goods were shipped in an open truck on a rainy day. This in itself helps you realize what your real problems are, and will allow corrective actions to be developed more readily.

From the diagram you can see that you have arranged your "causes" (shown as bars) in descending order of magnitude and can clearly see that Causes A and B are the most frequent (frequency being plotted on the left-hand y-axis). A clearer idea of how large a *proportion* of your problems are caused by A and B is shown by the single line marking the cumulative percentage of frequency (plotted on the right-hand y-axis). This simple diagram shows that 20 percent (2 out of 10) of your causes account for 67 percent of your reasons for dissatisfaction. Not quite 80 percent, as this is not a perfect world, but you can clearly see the impact of just two causes. And see how silly it would be to eliminate Cause J first—it barely accounts for 2 percent of your problems.

So, you've found your biggest problems and have been persuaded that you tackle just those to have maximum effect. How do you know that the steps you took to correct these have been effective? Simple—collect similar data after you have taken corrective action and replot a Pareto diagram. Have Causes A and B disappeared to the end of the line where I and J were? If so, you've been successful (and exceedingly so if they've disappeared altogether). If not, at least the diagram tells you so and stops you blindly carrying on in the belief that your corrective action has been effective.

And now to the basic question "Why should I aim for perfection?" The Six Sigma Approach to quality is promoted by the Motorola Company and adopted by many others—such as IBM, Xerox, and Boeing. Sigma (using the symbol σ, a Greek letter), also known as the standard deviation, is a measure of how much your values differ from an ideal value. The smaller your sigma is, the tighter control over your process you have. Without getting too complicated, the Six Sigma approach means that provided a process is controlled to plus or minus six sigma of your ideal value, everything that falls within these limits would pass, and it would only produce 3.4 defects per million. Not bad, you say!

Dr. Taguchi disagrees with this concept of "conforming to specification limits" and instead has a philosophy that we should aim for the smallest variation around our ideal value. Not only does this make sense, he has shown that by decreasing variation, costs also decrease. If variation and costs are reduced, the performance and quality of that performance will automatically improve. Important to customer service is Taguchi's philosophy that associates "loss of quality" not only with product quality, but also with customer dissatisfaction, which can lead to market share loss.

Taguchi's Quality Loss Function (QLF) indicates that loss continually increases as a produce or service deviates from your goal:

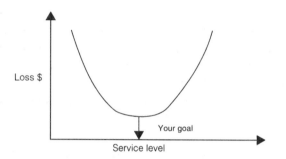

The QLF curve is quadratic, which in simple terms means that loss increases by the square of the distance from your goal. More dramatically stated, if your deviation is doubled, your loss is quadrupled, and if your deviation is tripled, your loss is multiplied nine times! A sure way of convincing one and all that you should aim for perfection . . . always!

3   What is measured, is done

Thanks to Liz Burrows for that case study.

It is important to measure the success of any service quality strategies. What is measured, is done.

Without measurements to determine whether your company is making tangible improvements, it is possible to spend significant amounts of money on service and not know if it has been wisely invested.

Measurements must be specific to each organization and measure what you want to measure. If you wish to determine customer satisfaction levels on the timeliness of response to letters, you first need to determine what the current time frame is. Once you know the number of days, you can then set standards for improvement and monitor progress against the original benchmark; regardless of how high or low it may be.

Federal Express is an American transport company that gained tremendous market share by promising customers overnight delivery. When first introduced, that promise fell well short of expectations but because they were still more reliable than the postal system, they managed to grow and prosper. They continually monitored their progress, which rapidly improved to a level of 98 percent of deliveries actually being made overnight. When the CEO was interviewed, the media were astounded that he wasn't satisfied with this. He said: "I can't be happy with 98 percent because that means more than 6,000 customers are not getting their parcels absolutely on time overnight and I won't be happy until they do!"

If the blood banks delivered only 98 percent of blood needed in a day, many people's lives would be at risk.

In a clothing shop in Connecticut, the cash register attendant asks whether or not the customer was helped by a salesperson that day. If so, the sales clerk's name is entered at the point of sale. It is a means of tracking who is, or is not, actively helping customers and staff realize that if they don't meet minimum standards, then they risk their jobs. And there is no ambiguity as to what standards they are being measured on.

General Norman Schwarzkopf emphasized the importance of setting high standards and measuring against them. At one early stage in his military career, he was placed in charge of helicopter maintenance. He asked how much of the fleet was able to fly on any given day. The answer was always 75 percent. It was never 74 percent or 76 percent, but 75 percent because that was the standard that had previously been set.

Schwarzkopf decided to establish a new standard of 85 percent and sure enough, within a short period of time, the response was that 85 percent of helicopters were available to fly (*Success* magazine 1991). And yes, the standard was again reset! That's what leaders do.

Books dedicated to total quality control contain detailed information on sophisticated measurement processes. I'm totally committed to the quality movement and measurement of improvement, but I believe too many people can become alienated by the introduction of overly complicated measurements. If these become too complex, employees feel they are engaging in measurement for measurement's sake and lose sight of what was meant to be achieved by such measurement. So, overly zealous statistical analysis should be avoided unless there are clearly defined outcomes and benefits to everyone. Weighing yourself 10 times a day doesn't change your weight. Nor does buying an expensive scale!

Measurements must also be relevant to the customer. In one *Yes Minister* episode (a BBC television series), a hospital was shown where there had been dramatic improvements in efficiency. The statistics were impressive by any measure until it was discovered there were no actual patients in the hospital because that would reduce their performance measures!

Stanley Marcus, the founder of Neiman Marcus retail stores, many years ago had an interesting observation on measurement by stating:

Consumers are statistics. Customers are people.

4 Service guarantees

Service guarantees can give companies a competitive edge. Customers like to know what they can expect and to be guaranteed that level of service.

Domino's home delivery pizza gained significant market share by being the first to guarantee delivery within 30 minutes or the customer received a $3 discount. In many hotels now, if your breakfast order doesn't arrive within five minutes of the appointed time, it's on the house. Some banks followed suit by guaranteeing that customers wouldn't need to stand in a line longer than seven minutes. If you did, you'd receive $5 cash. This worked for some banks as their service levels improved, but backfired on others.

Another bank was losing business because of constant errors in customer statements. The new manager sent a letter to customers explaining he would give $10 for every incorrect statement brought into the bank. The board thought it was a recipe for disaster because of the number of errors. The bank paid out significant sums of money within the first few weeks, but when the manager received an incorrect statement, he found out the reason behind it. Was it a computer error? Was it entered incorrectly? Was the teller's handwriting illegible? By focusing on the problem, error rates soon reduced and customer satisfaction and business increased.

A hospital in the United States guarantees you won't have to wait more than 20 minutes to be admitted. If you do, you receive 25 percent off your hospital bill, which is a significant amount under the American health care system.

Organizational efficiency and public accountability are improved by these methods. They also win customers' respect.

Whenever giving service guarantees, it is best to be as specific as possible. For example, state that you will attend to a service call "within two hours" not merely "as soon as possible." In one advertisement Nissan told customers about "The Nissan Satisfaction Commitment," the new three-year warranty, a 24-hour roadside assistance service, and a customer call line open 24 hours a day, 365 days of the year.

Other automobile manufacturers offered a similar, but less publicized, guarantee as some felt it may imply that the cars were unreliable if you focused on breakdowns.

One major telecommunications carrier announced that: "Customers will receive a rebate on their bill if we fail to provide the promised service."

Service guarantees can also be applied to internal customers. Another example relates to a hotel manager in Minneapolis who heard complaints from housekeepers that the supply room kept running out of window cleaner and sponges. So he developed a guarantee that any housekeeper who couldn't get needed supplies on any given day would get $5 from the supply department. This exercise cost the hotel $2,200 but produced a more efficient system of ordering and lowered housekeeper turnover.

Service guarantees can even apply to education. One New York high school actually guarantees employers certain standards of literacy and numeracy for their graduates. Those students who fail to meet employer expectations return to school for remedial evening classes, at no cost to the employer. Many employers make this conditional upon the student keeping their job!

The amazing thing is that the manufacturer (that is, the school) that offers the return of "faulty products" has not yet had a case in which an employer has taken advantage of the offer. This is due to the fact that the school focuses on certain quality standards during the education process and is therefore confident of their end result. This differs from most educational institutions in that the employer, not the school, decides if the student is properly educated.

This is why I always offer a 100 percent money-back guarantee on my presentations. My bank manager was horrified at this thought when I first established my business (as cash flow is always an issue for any business). But, I'm sure it helped attract more business, by engendering confidence in what was an "unknown brand name" at that time and has now afforded me the opportunity to ski at resorts that even offer money-back guarantees if there's no snow! On one such trip to New Zealand, I noticed a brochure for fly-fishing. Their "No fish—no pay!" guarantee seemed like great bait for customers!

A final word on service guarantees—what not to do. This sign appears on the side of a dumpster in Nambucca Heads, New South Wales: "Satisfaction guaranteed or double your garbage back!" Hardly an incentive to deal with them!

5   Add value by doing that little bit extra

It's important that all employees realize that customer care is about more than simply "doing their job." They must recognize it's about going that little extra distance to add value and exceed customer expectations. Let's look at some practical examples.

John Good, an executive with Mercedes-Benz in Singapore, was full of praise about exceptional service he received from the staff of an airline in relation to an issue that had absolutely nothing to do with the airline. It's an excellent example of caring about your customer. John landed at Sydney airport and needed to get to the Blue Mountains, a two-hour drive. Mercedes provided a car, but there was no street map. He tentatively asked one of the airline staff if they might be able to point him in the right direction. Much to his surprise, a young man was finishing his shift and not only pointed him in the right direction but, as he was going part of the way, had John follow him to the freeway, giving directions should they become separated. As a discerning customer and provider of excellent service himself, John couldn't help but be impressed.

My own personal favorite airline experience (and flying more than half a million miles per year, I have many!) occurred on a flight from Sydney to Canberra. I thought I would have ample time if I left Sydney at 2 p.m. for my 6 p.m. presentation to 300 small business owners at the National Convention Center. It's normally a 40-minute flight, but I always like to be early and allow for delays. So, I wasn't overly concerned when the 2 p.m. flight was canceled and I was rebooked on the 3 p.m. as that should still have had me on the ground at 3:40 for a 15-minute taxi ride to the venue, and still have a couple of hours to spare. However, I did become concerned when the 3 p.m. flight had a mechanical fault while on the runway and an hour later, we still hadn't moved. I was stuck . . . unable to change airlines or even use my cell phone. My first impulse was to panic, but I knew that wouldn't help so I enlisted the help of the flight attendant and outlined my problem, giving him a copy of my book *The Customer Service Zoo* and empathizing that he must feel like it was a zoo at the airport on a day like this. I told him how embarrassing it would be for a best-selling author on customer service to be late for an audience! He understood completely and arranged for the pilot to radio the ground staff with a message to call my client on their cell phone and outline the situation so they could, in the worst-case scenario, swap the order of presenters. The flight attendant then assured me that he was pretty sure we'd get there in the nick of time if I didn't have any luggage. But of course I not only had a huge suitcase with books, tapes, and videos for sale but my high heels were in the same suitcase . . . and I was horrified at the thought of addressing a professional group in my walking shoes!

"Don't worry," the flight attendant assured me, "you just jump in a taxi and I'll wait for your luggage and follow about ten minutes behind so you'll have the books by the conclusion of the talk." He then inquired what size of shoe I wore and asked the female flight attendants if anyone was an 8½. Alas, no such luck, but I'd already decided not to worry about that as my only concern was getting to the presentation at all. He assured me that I would and then reported that the pilot had been in touch with the client and they would have a car waiting at the airport and that the ground crew was in contact with the client to let them know the exact takeoff time of the plane, when it was half way and within five minutes of touchdown. With this out-standing service, I felt like a cross between Cinderella and a Federal Express package! In addition, I was able to use this example in my pres-entation, which I was only five minutes late for. It was a great "real time" case study of how this young man had comprehended and cared about my situation.

Another example is a classic. A rather scruffily dressed bank cus-tomer visited his local branch with his dog, as he had done for many years. The bank had recently undergone renovations and staff curtly informed this long-standing customer that his dog could not come in, as it had done in the past. A debate followed and the man withdrew more than $500,000 and walked across the street to another bank.

Overlooking his tatty clothes to see the true value of the cus-tomer, the staff not only let his dog enter, but one of them went to a nearby shop to buy the dog some biscuits. The customer was thrilled with this gesture.

The employee of the competitive bank, who told me this story, ended cynically by saying that each bank thrives on the incompe-tency of the other banks. It's the same for any business!

During a visit lasting more than a week to the Centra Hotel in Melbourne's World Trade Centre, I accumulated a large number of newspapers that I'd piled in one corner, as there were a few articles I wished to extract. One day, an overly zealous housekeeper threw out back editions of the papers. When I noticed this and called the front desk, a young man called Christopher listened carefully and asked if I could recall which newspapers contained the articles I wished to keep. I told him it was the Tuesday or Wednesday edition of *The Australian*.

"Don't worry," he replied. "My parents will have that at home and if you can wait until tomorrow, I'll bring in those copies."

That young man certainly cared about his customer and was willing to do something that wasn't in his job description. Congratu-lations Christopher!

Medical practitioners are also providers of service and need to genuinely care about their patients. Yet, one hears countless stories about indifference. Doctors need to not only listen and acknowledge the intelligence of their clientele, but should have time to see patients in an emergency without keeping others waiting unnecessarily. Going that extra distance goes a long way.

There are many stories of exceptional service. From Sydney airport's long-term parking area, a courtesy coach takes passengers to and from the air terminal. They have designated pick-up and drop-off points but on one rainy day, the driver drove a pregnant woman and child to her car and he put her luggage in the trunk. He then drove every other passenger to their cars . . . going that extra distance, literally and figuratively.

Following one of my radio programs, I received a letter from a listener who had just become a first-time father. He couldn't wait to tell me about Milton Pharmaceutical.

His wife had purchased a bottle-sterilization unit. As new parents, they admitted total responsibility for damaging the lid of the equipment. By 3 p.m. that day, they not only had a lid delivered to their door but a complimentary pack of sterilization tablets! All this was done by Milton Pharmaceutical even though it was entirely the fault of the customer. Obviously, those parents will be brand loyal to Milton for life and Milton no doubt hopes they continue procreating and telling all their friends of similar child-producing years! That's customer care!

All kinds of businesses are adding value to their traditional services. Some funeral directors now call the bereaved frequently for a few weeks after the burial and provide grief counseling and financial planning (if requested) all as part of the service.

On one occasion, in need of some wire for picture frames at home, I happened to cycle past a local gallery in Sydney. Wanting only a couple of feet of wire, I was astonished when the proprietor refused to accept any payment for such a small amount. What's more, she never batted an eyelid at the fact that my cycling pants, t-shirt, and safety helmet were not the normal attire in the gallery. The result being that six months later, I returned and placed an order for more than $4,000 worth of framing on behalf of my business—this time in corporate attire!

Nice guys don't finish last! Caring about customers pays.

It's passion that leads suppliers to add value. As a customer, I often have pretty definite views about what I want and I don't appreciate some high-powered salesperson trying to dissuade me to a different point of view. However, I certainly do value it when I sense they are listening carefully and fully comprehending my requirements, while gently offering suggestions on enhancements. Two examples come readily to mind.

One was an instance when I wished to produce some audiocassettes. A couple of producers gave quotes as per my specifications, but one did far more. He took the time to ask questions and showed a genuine interest in my project. He offered suggestions and diplomatically challenged some false assumptions I had made. As a result, we established an excellent working partnership and more so, I know the final product was much better than if it had been done exactly to my specifications. He truly added value by bringing his expertise to bear.

A local printer did the same with a poster I wanted produced. Rather than simply take the job order to run off the required copies, they suggested lamination, which I had not even considered. Yes, it cost more money but was a much better solution . . . a classic win/win scenario because some customers don't always know the services that you can offer to give them an even better solution to their initial needs.

Caring about customers is not only about fixing their problems as required. It's about doing something for them when they least expect it. Or it's about making them feel good by doing something extra.

Antlers Doubletree Hotel, in Colorado Springs, gave the impression that they really care. Not only did I receive freshly baked chocolate chip cookies when I arrived, but the front desk made a point to write a personalized "Customer care" number on the front of my keycard and made it clear I could call that number any time day or night with any request. It's actually no different to calling the front desk—it's simply packaged as a genuine attempt to care about the traveler.

Whenever I think about genuinely caring about customers, the words of my father echo in my ear: "It's not what you say but the way you say it." This maxim is especially true when (not if!) you're having a difficult customer or a bad day. It's so easy to let body language or tone of voice show your own frustration. You can't afford to let this happen with your employees and expect customers to believe you're sincere in wanting to help them with their problem.

Studies have shown that only a small percentage of understanding comes from the words used—most is inferred from tone of voice, posture, gestures, and facial expressions. Make sure employees don't unconsciously raise an eyebrow, fold arms menacingly in front of them, look away from their listener, sigh, yawn, tap fingers, or engage in any other distracting behavior.

Create loyal fans

Every employee must realize that genuine customer care cannot be faked. It's much more than mouthing one of those often referred to and insincere "Have a nice day" comments. It's much more than attending some course on customer service. Think, for example, of the service in your local pharmacy and then read the following.

A dear friend of mine, Michael Wrublewski, was the founding chairman and owner of the Sydney Kings and Flames pro basketball teams. He was previously a pharmacist by profession and built his business by making sure the chemistry is right for all his customers, be they large corporate sponsors or people who need a prescription delivered to their home.

A successful businessman with a range of ventures in Australia and overseas, he still found time to serve behind the counter in the first drugstore he ever opened.

His philosophy on customer service was the cornerstone of his success. Whenever he hired people for his drugstores, he always told them they must, at all times, with no exception whatsoever, be pleasant to customers and put a smile on their faces. He simply said: "People who go to a pharmacy are usually already sick and don't want to see a frown behind the counter."

This same customer focus transformed the growth of basketball in Australia. A number of years ago the Sydney Kings were lucky to get 400 spectators at an old stadium in an industrial area of town. During the transformation, they regularly packed the Sydney Entertainment Centre with more than 10,000 loyal fans. That certainly is the challenge of any business . . . to turn customers into your biggest fans!

How did Wrublewski effect such a dramatic transformation with a fledgling sporting team? First, he changed the focus from concentrating purely on the male-dominated sports aspect to redirecting the focus to an evening of entertainment for the entire family.

He provided an environment that was clean and alcohol-free. He arranged half-time entertainment and nonstop action, even during one-minute breaks in the game. He involved the crowd and referred to them as the sixth person on the team, assuring them that their participation was vital to encouraging the five players on the court.

The success of the basketball organization wasn't overnight. They first moved from their 400-seat stadium to a slightly larger one. As crowds continued to grow it came time to move to the Entertainment Centre. Loyal fans said that they probably wouldn't go to games anymore because parking was so expensive. Listening to his past customers, Wrublewski negotiated parking arrangements so as not to disadvantage the fans who had been the base of Kings' support in the past. What's interesting is that, at the time of publication, the men's team still haven't won a national title, and even with changes in management, plus good and bad publicity, the Kings and Flames have still maintained many loyal fans and a solid bottom line for their organization. Now they play at the Olympic site.

That's caring enough about customers to focus on the so-called "little" things it takes to keep them coming back. As a pharmacist, Mike knew that the best sort of business is repeat business. And, when he, as the original owner, first convinced a television station to televise part of a game, he asked fans to move to the opposite side of the stadium to face the cameras, as he knew viewers would be more excited about basketball if it looked as if others were passionate about the game. Success breeds success.

When asked about the phenomenal growth of the Kings, Wrublewski would reply: "There's no secret. It's simply about listening to the customer and then giving them what they want." Like a doctor, he believed in the need to first listen to the patient's problem before attempting to diagnose a remedy.

"First find out what they want. And then give it to them. Or suggest something that may be even better."

Yet, how often do we not really listen to customers . . . or others? How often do we ask a stranger on the street for directions and only hear part of what they say?

Caring about customers is essential in the good times and the bad times; probably even more so in hard times. Remember the old saying: "Tough times don't last. Tough people do!"

Clients don't just want fair-weather suppliers. There's never a better opportunity to add value than when helping a customer in trouble. Not enough sales representatives share the long-term perspective because traditionally they have been rewarded purely on monthly, quarterly, or yearly revenue results. The successful salesperson of the future will realize it's not a trade-off between results and customer care, but a direct correlation.

Even if you have hundreds of customers, you must work at treating everyone as an individual. One challenge is to have service representatives write "personal" customer letters that don't appear word-processed and contain all the relevant information.

It's acceptable to have a "shell" document with the pertinent information. It should be in simple English and in the active, not the passive, voice. For example, rather than say: "That matter is being handled by . . . " state: "Someone will handle that complaint."

Address the specific concern of the customer and acknowledge it. It also helps to insert the customer's name in the main body of the letter to personalize it.

6 Tips on tipping

It must have only been seconds but it seemed an eternity as I waited for the rear, left-hand door of the taxi to open at the airport. As if that wasn't bad enough, the cab driver commented on the fact that I didn't join him in the front.

"Expectin' company are ya, lady?" he asked sarcastically.

Welcome back to America, I thought, as I apologetically justified my actions as a result of living in Japan for the last two years. As he inconsiderately exhaled smoke backwards, I reminisced of the "good old days"; only nine hours removed but light years away in service standards.

On my way to the airport in Tokyo, I sat on pristine seat covers, which belied their constant use. I never needed to endure the political or sporting leanings of the driver. How could I ever explain to this driver that the last taxi I rode in was driven by a man with white gloves who bowed as I left?

"What about a tip?"

Oh yes, I'd forgotten that too after my experience in Japan.

"I'll give you a tip . . . courteous service."

Not all taxi drivers are the same. I have discovered some who give excellent service.

- I can phone and book in advance.
- They arrive on time.
- Their cabs are clean.
- They are polite.
- They know the best routes.
- They help with luggage.
- They don't drive too fast, while still being sensitive to time.
- They have air-conditioning.
- They have car phones.
- They respect the customer's choice to chat or remain silent.
- They don't have loud music or dispatch operators blaring.

And their service doesn't cost a cent more!

One driver claims that business has increased 60 percent since the installation of 24-hour cell phones and pagers. Most of their bookings are now direct so they gain the added benefit of reducing personal danger to themselves by knowing their clientele.

Tipping

Tipping is a factor in many service industries.

When should customers tip? Why is a tip expected in a taxi but not a bus, when both are forms of public transport? Why does a waitress or waiter expect a tip, when a flight attendant does not, when both serve food? And, why do customers feel intimidated to tip in certain situations and not others?

I have experienced a clone of *Fawlty Towers*, a BBC comedy series, or worse. The service was inept and the food barely edible. Despite our at-first polite protestations at the quality of the appetizer, the service and food didn't improve at all for the main course. We decided to go elsewhere for dessert. The bill was paid with the exact amount of money. On a paper napkin I wrote: "I used to be a waitress and usually leave a tip but in this instance the only tip I can give is to provide friendlier and more efficient service!"

To have left a tip would only have reinforced poor service behaviors; there was little likelihood of improvement in general service standards.

If service is good, a tip is appropriate. However, in Australia, there is no social or moral obligation to do so if the service is mediocre. Nor should there be elsewhere, although I am sympathetic to different wage structures in North America and appreciate that waiting staff need to make a fair living. After all, I was a waitress for four years but still firmly believe that tipping needs to be a matter of choice and that choice surely must rest with the customer.

We have probably all experienced extreme contrasts in service. In some hotels, for example, we are overexposed to information that is readily available and we yearn for solitude. Yet the "do not disturb" notice will be ignored. In other hotels, we are welcomed, asked if anything is needed, and left to take the initiative in the future. Which service would you prefer?

Some people give personalized service and customer care, but never linger for a tip. Some people deserve tips, and some establishments deserve acknowledgment of that little extra care. Here is an example from one such hotel.

- There was a personalized welcome letter and bowl of fruit from the manager.
- There was remote control on the television as well as complimentary videos to borrow.
- There was herbal tea as well as standard tea and coffee.
- There was an array of magazines.
- There was a bathrobe.
- There was turndown service with chocolates.
- There was a shoehorn and umbrella on loan.
- They had quality wooden coat hangers to hang in the shower to steam clothes.
- They had a powerful hair drier.
- Pagers were available at no charge.
- When I booked a wake-up call, the operator double-checked the pronunciation of my name.
- They put the morning newspaper under the door to save naked guests the embarrassment of retrieving it from the hall.
- They advertised they had access to a drugstore that would deliver at all hours.
- They had shopping bags in the rooms.
- And, they even had bathroom scales, which I'm sure were diplomatically set to weigh a little on the light side!

One would expect all these extra amenities and extended services to cost substantially more than another hotel only two blocks away, which provided none of the above. Yet, there was only a $10 variation on the room rate.

One different perspective on caring and the effect it can have on good service . . . You often receive better service if you make a little effort to go out of your way to be nice to the service provider, rather than expect them automatically to be nice to you. In an ideal service environment, the onus for initiating this rapport should be on the service provider, but from a consumer's point of view, it can often make the experience more pleasant if you are pleasant to begin with. If everyone started treating others in a more courteous manner, it could snowball.

In a motor vehicle repair shop in Melbourne is this sign:

Service rates:
 $30 per hour if mechanic repairs
 $40 per hour if you give advice
 $50 per hour if you want to help

Whether large or small, private or public sector—regardless of subsequent changes within the organization—we all need to give genuine customer care, not simply to win an award, but more important) to win customers for life.

On a flight to Bangkok, I noticed an advertisement for Thai Airlines, which read: "Smooth as silk service from the heart—not the handbook."

How true! Certainly one can learn from procedures in the handbook and I'm certainly not adverse to handbooks (quite the contrary as standardization is important) But, we need to combine the handbook and the heart; the head and the heart.

Using one's heart as well as one's head was demonstrated on another visit to New Zealand. While training to cycle over the Andes, I tried to hire a bicycle but it was winter and the rental shops were closed. However, the young concierge at the hotel delighted me the next day by bringing in his own bike from home. There was nothing in the handbook about that!

My all-time best personal experience of genuine customer care occurred at a hotel in Perth and formed the basis for another best-selling book, *Hot Lemon & Honey . . . Reflections For Success in Times of Change*.

When I started speaking professionally, I believed I could make money and make a difference. However, like most burgeoning business owners, I was occasionally plagued with doubt. Once was after a long flight, when I arrived with no voice, to address 400 realtors the next morning (an occupational hazard indeed!).

At hotel check-in, the receptionist started her standard greeting, outlining the magnificent facilities, but I cut her short with a whisper, to say that I simply wanted to get to my room immediately. I promptly unpacked, showered, and curled up in bed, feeling somewhat sorry for myself away from home, when I heard an unexpected knock at the door.

"Room service."

I croakily informed him that I hadn't ordered room service.

"Yes, Ms. DeVrye, we know you haven't ordered room service but we *also* know you're not feeling well, so have brought some hot lemon and honey with our compliments."

Sure enough, on a silver tray, was exactly what I would have wanted if I'd been home. In addition, there was a handwritten note from the chef offering to make chicken soup and another note from the concierge, with some vitamin C tablets and an offer to obtain any additional medication from the drugstore in town.

As someone who spends more than 80 nights per year in five-star hotels, I know that sort of service isn't standard, nor in anyone's job description. The receptionist put herself in my shoes and coordinated others to deliver outstanding service. I felt better already and naturally, any traveler would remember that experience long after the marble in the foyer was forgotten!

My voice marginally restored the next day, I addressed the real estate agents and used this real-time example of going that extra mile to truly care about the customer. I'd arranged for the receptionist to attend the presentation, and later, at check-out, she said she felt somewhat stunned by the spontaneous applause from the audience, saying, "Just to know that you felt better made me feel better about my day. I didn't expect any thanks." By doing that little extra, she gained extra satisfaction for herself.

I'm pleased to report that the real estate company adopted *Hot Lemon & Honey* service as their annual theme, achieving record profits that year. Subsequently, *Hot Lemon & Honey . . . Reflections For Success in Times of Change* became the title for another book.

Remember this receptionist when you get up and head off to work each day. Will someone so fondly recall you for making a difference? Because, in spite of the frustration we all experience in our daily tasks, isn't it reassuring to remember that we too truly can make our life worth living as our living is being made?

Here's another example I read on the front page of a leading Australian newspaper:

> *A visitor booked into a hotel minus his baggage lost in transit. He had a suit but no shoes as he'd traveled in sneakers [see, I'm not the only one who does so!]. He had an important meeting the next morning but it wasn't a problem as the young man at reception wore the same size of shoe, which he offered to the guest. While the well-shod guest attended his meeting, the hotel employee went out and bought another pair for him!*

Now that's truly putting yourself in the customer's shoes; or vice versa. And what a delightful contrast to the following story told about customers arriving at a busy restaurant and giving their name to the maître d'.

After a while, people who arrived after them were being shown their tables. "Why is it that we've been kept waiting when we were here first?" asked the customer.

The maître d' with his nose in the air, looked down the waiting list and pointed at their name, which had a line through it. "Madam," he resounded pompously, "you have already been seated!"

If you've ever treated a customer like that, please go back and reread this chapter on care!

S E V E N   K E Y   P O I N T S
in this chapter on caring:

1 You never win an argument with a customer.

2 User-friendly operations make it easy for customers to do business with you.

3 99 percent error-free isn't good enough when striving for quality.

4 What is measured, is done. Don't be afraid to set high standards of excellence.

5 Add value by doing a little bit extra.

6 Listen to the customer. Use your head and your heart for best results.

7 In my own organization, I will improve service through caring by:

_____

_____

_____

_____

_____

_____

_____

■ SELF-ESTEEM

■ EXCEED EXPECTATIONS

■ RECOVER

■ VISION

■ IMPROVE

■ CARE

7 Empowerment

*Give a man a fish for a day
and he eats for a day.
But, teach him to fish
and he eats for a lifetime.*

—Anonymous

Empowerment is more than delegation. It's about teaching employees "how to fish."

- You teach them to fish by providing basic training in product knowledge and other specific technical information relevant to the business.
- You encourage them to fish by creating a work environment of trust and mutual respect to produce high individual self-esteem and team morale.
- You motivate them to fish by creating a vision of service excellence and providing constructive counseling when those standards aren't met.
- You encourage them to take ownership of their own fishing hole and equipment; to feel responsible for the end result.

And then, you let them fish! You let them make decisions that relate directly to the customer. After all, they're certainly in the best position to do so.

1 Make employees responsible and response-able

Empowerment entails having employees feel responsible for the outcomes in the organization. The ultimate objective is to have them feel that every action they take is what they would do if they owned the business. And, to do this, they have to understand that they first "own" the complaint.

If employees are to feel truly responsible, the organization must have a climate that also makes everyone feel response-able. There should be few barriers to prevent people from acting in a responsible manner.

Does your organization have unnecessary procedures and bureaucratic rules?

Be honest! Certainly it is necessary to have certain procedures and this varies with the nature and size of the operation. But how many bureaucratic procedures are in place that aren't required? Were some introduced many years ago and remained long after their usefulness has been served?

Jan Carlzon, CEO of Scandinavian Airlines, asked all employees to focus on minor improvements in their own area of the operation. He made staff responsible and response-able. It used to take no fewer than nine signatures on a form to enable a flight attendant to provide extra coffee and cookies if the plane was delayed. Yet, who was in the best position to determine whether or not it was appropriate to serve customers extra amenities during the delay? The flight attendant!

Carlzon eliminated the nine signatures on the form, reducing the workload of eight people and significantly reducing the frustration of the person at the front line who had to put up with unnecessary red tape.

Carlzon went further and said if the attendants wished to give champagne and caviar to the business clientele, that was also accept-able. Most of middle management thought this was a recipe for disaster and didn't credit flight attendants with the necessary judgment. Certainly, if attendants had provided champagne when a flight was delayed a few minutes, the airline would have been in more financial difficulty. But, they did act responsibly and only provided the extra amenities if, in their opinion, it was warranted to appease passengers.

Is it possible that middle management saw the elimination of the nine signatures as a threat to their own jobs and sense of importance? The fact of the matter is that most employees would rather give good service than mediocre or poor service.

Unfortunately, not all employees or employers share that sense of excellence. I'd come home exhausted one rainy Friday evening and both the plane and the luggage arrival were extremely late. Although frustrated, I wasn't at all upset with the airline as I understood the adverse weather conditions and that Friday night was their peak travel time and was certain that they were doing their best in difficult circumstances.

The next day I had another flight with the same airline on a bright sunshiny Saturday morning. As the plane sat on the runway for 20 or so minutes, with no apparent reason for a delay, I politely inquired as to what was causing the delay. "Oh, catering has screwed up again," the flight attendant snapped. "There's a Muslim family on board and catering forgot their special meal."

I'm sure she said it to deflect any blame from her, without realizing that by knocking other members of her airline team, she made herself look bad as well.

After another 20 minutes had passed, we were still sitting there and the flight attendant was obviously also distressed, so I quietly suggested that it was only a one-hour flight so why didn't she act empowered and offer the family a free meal voucher in a restaurant at the other end, an upgrade on their next flight, or some other form of compensation? I even joked that they could have the vegetarian meal I'd ordered for that day, because in terms of priorities, it seemed silly to hold up a plane of 200 people because a special meal was missing for four passengers, for a one-hour flight, although it may have been a problem for a longer flight. She looked at me as if I had two heads and responded: "I've already offered them free drinks, according to our guidelines."

As I patiently pointed out that Muslims don't drink alcohol and she should consider another solution, she told me in no uncertain terms that she was "in charge" of the in-flight service! Ha! She wouldn't have a clue about the meaning of the word and as the plane was now three-quarters of an hour late for a one-hour flight, my patience had worn thin!

By the time I arrived to speak at a conference, I asked how many other people had experienced delayed flights on that airline and most of the room put up their hands. I then explained that this was simply because one flight attendant had checked her brains in when she arrived at work that day and wouldn't use common sense, so not only was my flight delayed, but so too was the return flight and then the next flight going back to the conference destination and so on. The domino effect of that dumb decision affected not just the customers but her co-workers all day long!

I later found out, by talking to staff on the return flight, that there were, in fact, other options available to them in such situations but, apparently this particular flight attendant chose not to use them.

Be part of the solution—not part of the problem

It's one thing if frontline personnel have the ability to use their good judgment and another if they consistently face irate customers because of errors and policies beyond their control. If it's the latter, they naturally become frustrated and disillusioned. This can lead not only to a sense of apathy, but also to increased turnover and the additional cost of training new employees.

If employees feel they have some responsibility and are in a position to be able to help the customer, they are more likely to act in a responsible manner. It's very demeaning and demotivating if frontline personnel are burdened with a strict policy that they must implement, regardless of the situation. Many times, the frontline personnel know what should be done to create a win/win situation for the customer and the company. But the rulebook states that anything outside the norm must be referred to a supervisor, who has all too often insulated himself from the customers and the frontline staff. When the customer then explains the same problem to the supervisor, often the response is: "Oh yes, we can fix that."

The intonation in the voice often implies that the employee should have done so in the first place. This not only damages staff morale, but creates additional and unnecessary frustration and time delays for the customer.

> 70 percent of complaining customers will buy from you again if you resolve the problem in their favor.
>
> 95 percent will buy again if you resolve the problem on the spot.
>
> —Michael Le Boeuf, Ph.D.

I've also heard it estimated that 70 percent of customers are satisfied if they only need to deal with one employee to fix their complaint. If a second person is involved, the satisfaction rate drops to 61 percent and diminishes further if their complaint continues to be passed to someone else. By eliminating some unnecessary bureaucracy, you can create a better environment for both employees and customers.

Victa is a Melbourne-based company producing plastic injection molds. Quality control is a vital part of their operation to ensure strict adherence to specifications for molding. At one stage, three people were employed solely to inspect the finished products thoroughly, ensure faulty goods were not delivered to the customer, and to find the source of any problem. In spite of these rigid controls, major quality assurance problems continued.

In a change of strategy, Victa redeployed the three inspectors into the mainstream of the workforce. They announced to employees the three inspectors were being "fired" and more than 30 "inspectors" being hired in their place. The 30 inspectors were the existing workforce. Everyone was made to feel responsible for inspecting their own part of the work in progress. The "police" were eliminated. As a result, not only was there a decrease in reject products and an increase in overall quality, but absenteeism was significantly reduced.

Employees like to feel part of the solution . . . not part of the problem.

Contrast the Victa example to that of an unnamed public servant who recently sat next to me on a flight. He informed me he paid $450 for a return flight, compared with the $180 I paid. Rules within his department stated he must book seven days in advance through the internal travel department on a full economy fare.

"It's not only a waste of taxpayers' money, but I can't respond quickly to customer requests and then, they think it's me who is hopeless," he told me in frustration.

When asked why he didn't inform senior management, instead of me, about the obvious benefit of changing the rules in view of the intense airline competition, he responded: "It's no use telling the powers that be. They don't care what happens in the field and are only interested in creating rules to ensure they have something to do."

I quickly lost my original sympathy to his plight. If you're complaining about your company and don't bother to offer suggestions for improvement, you have no right to complain. If you're not part of the solution, you're part of the problem! (Bear in mind that management can't possibly implement every suggestion, so please don't be discouraged.)

2 Say yes instead of no

Many rules and regulations are essential for safety and/or financial reasons. But, many others serve only to inhibit initiative and productivity. If one must have rules, keep them as simple and uncomplicated as possible! Some employees could spend inordinate amounts of time interpreting and looking for loopholes in the rules, rather than simply getting on with the job.

Procedures and rulebooks aren't inherently bad. When used as a justification to say no to a customer, rather than looking for a creative solution to a customer problem and being able to say yes, they are obstructive.

For example, a few years ago, I had two amounts of cash deposited in separate term deposit accounts. I needed ready access to the funds to put a deposit on a property, so I called up the first bank and asked what procedure I needed to go through to withdraw the money.

"Don't you realize that you can't withdraw from a term deposit (dummy)," was the response of the teller. Admittedly she didn't actually use the word "dummy" but her tone of voice certainly implied it!

I then called the second financial institution where the person on the other end of the phone, at my credit union, responded politely: "Certainly Ms. DeVrye, we'd be happy to terminate that term deposit for you, but I'm obliged to tell you that you'll lose a significant proportion of interest for taking the funds out before the expiration date." I assured her I was aware of, and happy with, that penalty. I then called back the first bank and got a different teller. Sure enough, I could likewise withdraw funds with a similar loss of interest.

One financial institution came from a position of no and the other from a position of yes, but . . . It doesn't take a rocket scientist to know who I'll redeposit the funds with in the future! And, isn't it the same for any transaction in your organization? Always come from a position of *Yes, we can* to the customer, bearing in mind that both financial institutions mentioned had exactly the same policy.

3   Risk and learn from mistakes

Empowerment involves risk. Unfortunately, many middle-aged, middle-management personnel are inclined to exercise only caution! They have worked hard to get where they are and now see themselves as guardians of the status quo. Talk about empowering employees implies a loss of their hard-earned control.

Enlightened managers will realize that, with increased technology and specialization, it is no longer possible for any one person, regardless of personal genius, to be the guardian of all knowledge. This awareness of one's fallibility comes as a shock to managers who feel threatened by change and feel that knowledge is power.

Shared leadership is a prerequisite for successful organizations that wish to succeed in the 21st and 22nd centuries.

The concept of shared leadership is incorporated in a model, developed by Richard Foster of the world-renowned management firm, McKinsey. In his book *Innovation—The Attacker's Advantage*, he emphasizes the need for continual change in traditional management styles. Leaders of the future won't feel at all awkward in saying: "I don't know."

This is contrary to the traditional view that leaders should have all the answers. After all, they're the bosses and that's why bosses are paid. True leaders will recognize they are paid to bring out the best talents of every individual in the organization. The role of the leader is to motivate all employees to look continually for answers and for a better way to do things.

This is empowerment—relinquishing some of one's traditional, authoritative power to harness the energy of many others, producing a more powerful organization overall. Leaders of successful companies will recognize the whole is far greater than the sum of the parts when it comes to running an organization.

The irony is that the more empowered individuals feel, the more accumulative power goes back to the leader, who can share in the glory of a job well done by a motivated team.

Another risk of giving employees more responsibility is that they will inevitably make mistakes as they venture into new areas. That is a real risk that can't be avoided but can be managed. There is an old saying that a person who makes no mistakes makes nothing. Furthermore, the only way to get through life without making mistakes is to do nothing-and that is the biggest mistake of all.

People learn more from their mistakes than their successes—and employees are no exceptions to that rule. The role of the manager is to encourage employees to have a sound enough background of the business to feel confident to take a calculated degree of risk. For every decision, an employee should ask:

Would I be taking this risk if I owned the company?

If management encourages a spirit of mutual trust, treats employees with respect, and believes they will act responsibly, better decisions are likely to result. Naturally, management has an obvious role to reward risk that results in significant benefits to the organization; and also to offer constructive criticism when things don't go as planned.

When I worked for IBM, a story, apocryphal or not, circulated the ranks. It is the tale told of Tom Watson, founder of IBM, calling a young manager to his office. The young man had been responsible for a $10 million loss and, naturally, feared he would be fired. "No, I'm certainly not going to fire you," the CEO told him. "We have just invested $10 million in your education. Now, tell me what you have learned from that, which will help IBM?"

A top executive was quoted as saying: "If you haven't gotten into trouble lately for exceeding your authority, you're not doing your job."

Complacency can lead to a downturn in business. Newly established firms need to rely on risk-taking.

The benefits from employees taking risks far outweighs the downside resulting from honest mistakes made in the process.

Even if people are officially in the same role for a number of years, it's equally important, and often more difficult, to encourage them to step outside their comfort zones and try something new. This is more so when they are doing a basically "good job." It is important to encourage them to grow their job and grow with their job.

A good question to ask employees or yourself is: "Do you have ten years' experience in your job or two years' experience with eight years' of meaningless repetition?"

It's also risky to ask customers: "How are we doing? How could we do better?"

The risk is they might tell you. But with risk comes reward; and rewards come if staff elicit candid opinions from customers in order to make alterations and retain customers, before it's too late.

It's also important to ask your employees the same questions: "How is management doing? How could we do better?"

Again, the answers may not be what you want to hear—but you need to hear them.

It's essential that management informs employees of what's going on within the company. One can't expect staff to be empowered if they don't know the whole story. Management should share successes and problems. Employees may not want to hear bad news about the company's performance, but it's better to hear all the news directly from management than to rely on incomplete information from the rumor mill.

Risk is not the sole domain of the private sector and high-flying entrepreneurs. When it comes to customer service, no one is in a better position to take risks than government employees. Many have job security, so why not go out on a limb for a customer and be empowered to break a rule or two—if you believe it's the right thing to do for that particular customer in that particular situation!

4   Support and coach employees—the inverted management pyramid

It's important to remember that management can't expect employees to become instantly empowered. Empowerment takes considerable encouragement on the part of organizational leaders. It's akin to teaching your child to ride a bicycle. If the child falls over the first or second time, you don't say: "Well, that's it. I can see this isn't going to work. You'll never be able to ride a bike."

Quite the contrary. You encourage the child and make it possible for them to gain some confidence. It's the same with empowering employees. They need some support and encouragement from management, particularly in the early days. Some will need training wheels more than others. The key role of management is to articulate a common objective and then support employees in attainment of that goal.

The traditional management hierarchical structure is shaped like a pyramid with the boss at the top and employees at the bottom. Another way of looking at an organization is the inverted pyramid, where the most important people are symbolically displayed at the top of the organization. These are the customers. The next most important people are frontline personnel who interface with customers on a regular basis. Middle management appears below frontline personnel on the hierarchy, and the managing director is symbolized at the bottom of the organization chart.

This is not to say the buck doesn't still stop with the leader, but the reversed pyramid symbolizes to employees that they aren't at the bottom of the heap. Management's main role, based at the fulcrum, is to act in a supportive role to those at the broader end of the triangle. Figure 7.1 illustrates both the traditional and inverted pyramid structures.

As people become more empowered and technology provides a broader based distribution of knowledge to all employees, the triangular structure will flatten, as there is no longer a need for such depth in middle-management ranks.

Empowering employees can be likened to coaching a football team. A good manager, like a good coach, is not expected to play all positions on the field; to be everywhere and do everything. A good manager, like a good coach, will set objectives in advance. He or she will then provide training in basic skills to individual players and outline the objectives of their specific positions. The coach will encourage open communication among team members and go into a game confident that players have the basic skills and teamwork to be able to make an instantaneous decision on the field.

A good manager sets the direction and provides training in the basic skills. They then allow staff to run with the ball on the customer playing field.

Like a good coach, a good manager knows it won't happen overnight; that some individuals catch on more quickly than others. But a leader also recognizes that success breeds success and people

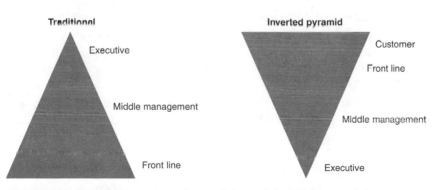

FIGURE 7.1 Two appproaches to hierarchical structure in an organization

generally wish to be identified with winning organizations, rather than losing ones.

A good manager recognizes the importance of providing encouragement to inspire team members to continually improve.

Dr. Ken Blanchard, author of *The One Minute Manager*, states that managers should:

> *Try to catch employees doing things right. Or, at least catch them doing things a little bit right and reward that behavior to spur them on to greater achievements.*

Coaches start at the bottom to encourage the desired result, little by little extending the scope and areas of responsibility. Acknowledging achievement helps the next move. If employees are praised whenever they improve their performance, they are more likely to strive further.

5 Incentives, recognition, and rewards

Too often, the only time staff hear from management is when they make a mistake!

We all have a need for recognition, to feel wanted and appreciated. Sir Colin Marshall, a chairman of British Airways, makes the point that it is important for all managers to recognize even the smallest achievements of staff: "Even if the achievement may seem small to you, it certainly isn't seen as small by those who achieved it."

Managers and supervisors should take note of this and practice recognizing achievement. High standards can lead to disappointment when they're not met. And yet significant improvements have been made and not rewarded.

"Thank you" are the two most under-used words in the modern management vocabulary. To set high standards and then praise people when they move toward achieving those standards is a much more potent strategy than treating customer service employees like cannon fodder at the front line.

Employee recognition need not be expensive. It does need to be recognized by others as an achievement. Peer recognition is very important, and so is the celebration of success. Can you imagine the significance of the Academy Awards if the recipients simply received a letter in the mail, informing them of their win? The Academy Awards are a gala celebration of success; the real power behind them is the tremendous peer presence and recognition on the evening.

If you wish to recognize the contribution of an employee, make sure it is a public celebration of their success—though not necessarily the length and expense of the Academy Awards. You could call co-workers together for morning coffee to say "thanks for a job well done" to a particular individual or team. Praise people in front of their peers—but offer constructive criticism in private to avoid embarrassing the individual.

Some might say: "The only thing that motivates employees is increased pay." There is no argument that if your organization pays competitively, compared with your industry standards, and your staff feel empowered, you have a better chance of attaining and retaining a more motivated workforce. But, contrary to public opinion, money isn't everything to today's workers.

Certainly, underpaying employees is a demotivator because most people rely on a certain level of income to maintain a desired lifestyle. However, annual salary increases are soon forgotten in the day-to-day working environment. They are seen as an expectation and not a motivator for more than a day or two.

One appliance manufacturer in the United States was amazed to discover that its employees were not more motivated by monetary rewards. They instigated a quality service program whereby employees were rewarded with "badges of honor" whenever they had done a particularly good job. Each badge had a monetary value and, at the end of the year, could be traded for product prizes from the company. For example, one badge might win a toaster, five a microwave, 10 a refrigerator, and so on. The management was amazed that more than 80 percent of employees did not turn in their badges for merchandise prizes, but chose to keep them publicly displayed at their workplace as a very visible and symbolic recognition of their contribution to the company! As a result of recognizing staff excellence in customer service, morale went up, absenteeism went down, profits went up, and everyone eventually ended up with a salary increase.

It is important that recognition should not become predictable nor an expectation. Many companies traditionally give employees a gift at Christmas. Initially seen as an expression of appreciation, such an act becomes an expectation of all staff, deserved or not.

Recognition becomes more powerful with immediacy. The sooner you can recognize an employee for an outstanding effort, the more powerful the effect upon that employee and others. Retail stores sometimes test customer service. Whenever the "tester" receives excellent service, he or she immediately hands a certificate to the employee. The employee's name is reported to management, who make a point of publicly recognizing the employee and giving a small monetary token of appreciation. This is done within 24 hours of the excellent service provision.

Management consultant Daniel Johnson shares what one of his clients is doing to ensure recognition at the front line:

> Jeffries Family Food Store is a suburban supermarket in North Croydon, Victoria. The managing director thinks cashiers are the most important people in his store. He knows they can make a customer's visit a good experience or guarantee a customer never returns. To enhance cashier loyalty and commitment to service, he has an overseas exchange program where the best cashiers are selected to work in an innovative supermarket in the USA. What a great incentive to one of the traditional lowly paid jobs.
>
> —(Johnson 1990)

Recognition of outstanding cashiers, or anyone else in your organization who goes that extra distance to provide service excellence, helps create "service heroes" within an organization. Smart management will go out of their way to create these heroes out of everyday employees. This can be done through presentations, certificates, posters, and using any internal means of employee communication such as bulletin boards and in-house newsletters and e-zines.

Champion teams

Many organizations recognize not only outstanding individual efforts but also offer incentives to teams who do a great job. One sales company reaped rewards from introducing team incentives for achievement of sales targets. End-of-year bonuses were given for reaching sales quotas, but if all members of a team met the quota, there was an added bonus. This created a greater spirit of cooperation, without undermining the significance of individual performance.

Too many sales staff are rewarded purely on short-term results. That's why some customers may be "oversold" and not inclined to do business with that organization in the future. Many sales organizations are now changing sales incentive plans. Frontline salespeople are not only rewarded for immediate revenue results, but also have a financial incentive based on surveys of customer satisfaction conducted 6, 12, or 18 months later. This sort of incentive provides the sales representative with a framework that emphasizes the company is interested in keeping customers for life and gaining repeat business. In the long run this produces better results than a single sale.

Recognition must not be given indiscriminately. Only those who do a good job should be rewarded. Recipients must be seen by their peers as truly deserving.

"Employee of the Month" awards can be valuable if the person has truly contributed more than others. It is rewarding for them to be recognized and possibly have their photograph publicly displayed. However, the danger with such schemes is the temptation to rotate the recognition, which degenerates into: "It must be so-and-so's turn to receive it this month." If you have such an award and one person deserves it three months in a row, then he or she should receive it three months in a row. The potency of such recognition is to set standards to which others can strive. It's important, when mentioning the recognition, to be specific and clearly outline why that particular individual is so deserving, so everyone else knows what management expects.

It's also important that employees value the sort of recognition you are proposing. Some rewards do nothing to improve service levels and actually have the opposite effect. It's imperative to first understand what kind of incentive will be seen as a real benefit to employees.

Although incentives should only be given to those who most deserve them, there is nothing wrong with saying "thank you" to all employees from time to time. The more innovative you can be in your expression of appreciation, the more likely it is to be appreciated.

Many years ago I managed a team of more than 200 staff and contractors throughout Australia, responsible for delivering technical education to IBM customers throughout Asia and the South Pacific. Our customer satisfaction surveys indicated we had significant improvements to make in our overall standard of educational service. I wrestled with various means to achieve this and decided to introduce an "Instructor of the Month" plan to recognize those teachers who received the highest customer satisfaction ratings that month. I was told it would never work because many of the staff were university lecturers and: "Academics don't fall for that sort of corny corporate motivation."

But I decided to introduce the program. Coincidentally, the next night, I chanced to see a movie titled *Dead Poets Society* and was inspired to write the following letter to all staff:

> *Dear (first name)*
>
> *I would like to extend an invitation to you and a partner to attend Dead Poets Society.*
>
> *So, what relevance does that have to Customer Education, you may well ask? The movie has a complex theme about human relations but many scenes revolve around a teacher who instills a desire to learn in his students. This teacher uses unconventional teaching methods. This teacher breaks with established norms. This teacher thinks outside the nine dots. He knows how to appeal to his audience. He is truly market driven in understanding what inspires them to learn. Need I say more?*
>
> *IF you and a friend would like to see it (it is not compulsory and does not have a happy ending), please be my guest. Simply submit your movie tickets on an expense sheet to your manager within 30 days.*
>
> *Even if you do not want to contemplate innovative teaching methods after hours, but would still like to see the movie, just think of it as a small thank you for the excellent work you are doing at present. We all have a lot of challenges to face between now and the end of the year, but we can look back on the first six months with a great deal of satisfaction and pride.*
>
> *THANKS!*

I then added a personalized, handwritten postscript to those staff I knew were excelling in their jobs.

I wasn't sure *what* reaction to expect   cynicism or bemusement.

I certainly did not expect a 22 percent improvement in customer satisfaction ratings the next quarter, but that's what happened! I was also delighted to see an improvement in staff morale.

The accounts department was far from delighted. They were horrified that I had given away movie tickets without filling in the necessary forms—even though that amount was well within my financial jurisdiction.

Often it's more effective to ask for forgiveness than permission when dealing with bureaucracies!

6 Make everyone a valuable team member

It's important to recognize that empowerment is not the sole domain of managers or professional staff. Successful organizations make everyone, regardless of status, feel empowered and able to make a difference.

Have you ever heard someone say "I only work here"?

How can you instill a feeling of worth in every employee? How can you make them feel part of the overall team and that, in spite of how "minor" they perceive their role to be, they all play a valuable part?

How can you get across the notion that the whole is, in fact, greater than the sum of the parts and it is essential for every employee, of every rank, to do their job to the highest standards?

A simple and effective analogy to impart to employees is that of a relay race, where they imagine the customer as the baton. In a relay race, each runner has the responsibility to do his or her best while carrying the baton; to add value with every step and give it their all-out effort until they pass the baton to another runner. But, as a member of a relay team, each runner has another responsibility. They must understand the strengths, weaknesses, and speed of the person from whom they receive the baton. They must also appreciate the strengths, weaknesses, and speed of the person to whom they pass the baton. All players must practice the smooth transition of the baton.

It's no different with customers; whether there are four people on an Olympic relay team or 40, 400, or 4,000 people on your organizational team, each person dealing with a customer must understand the limitations of the next department to which they refer the customer, if need be. If employees are on an assembly line, they must understand the entire chain of events required to turn out a quality product.

In short, there must be assurance that nothing slips through the cracks when a product or customer moves from one area of the business to another. Yet, how often do we hear people say: "Oh, I thought *they* were doing that"?

Admittedly, it takes time to practice the smooth transfer of the baton from one runner to another, just as it does the smooth transfer of a customer from one department to another. But the effort required to get the process right is well worth it.

Any team is only as strong as its weakest link. There can be record-breaking performances in many areas of an organization, but the race is lost if even one person drops the "customer baton."

This analogy of a relay race relates directly to the concept of internal customers. *Internal customers* are simply defined as others within your own organization who depend on you for completing a certain aspect of a product or process. Some people dismiss the concept of internal customers and claim the only real customer is the one paying the bill. Others refer to "Big C" customers as those who pay the bill and "Little c" customers as those who are internal customers. The important notion to convey is that employees often rely on others within the organization in order to do their job satisfactorily. So, it is imperative that everyone feels a sense of responsibility to ensure nothing slips through the cracks.

I'm totally committed to quality service, but that hasn't always been the case. It's only in recent years that I have fully appreciated the importance of everyone being part of the customer team. During my first year in Australia, I had a temporary job as a computer operator for Comalco's bauxite plant in Weipa, Queensland. After a couple of days on the job, I was charged with the responsibility of doing an all-night payroll run. My boss assured me nothing could go wrong, which I should immediately have taken as an ominous sign. I was left alone with the computer and something did go wrong about 4 a.m.

As a young new employee, I had no intention of waking my boss at that early hour. However, if I had understood the concept of the relay race, I wouldn't have hesitated. Because, at that particular moment, I was carrying the baton for the entire organization.

I didn't realize that if the payroll didn't get out, the mine workers were likely to strike. Bauxite wouldn't be loaded onto ships in the harbor. It wouldn't be transported to Gladstone to be processed into aluminum to then be manufactured into finished goods. It wouldn't be reloaded on ships to be exported. Revenues wouldn't then flow back into Australia to pay the salary of a lowly computer operator!

I wish someone had explained the simple concept of the relay race to me when I was young. You see, I wasn't a lowly computer operator at all, even though that's how I perceived myself. I was, indeed, carrying the baton for the entire Comalco company.

Fortunately, my boss arrived at 7 a.m. and we managed to avert disaster by getting the payroll out before the pub opened, which proved to be the key critical success factor!

Everyone is important

Everyone has an important role to play and must recognize that their valuable contribution, no matter how small it may seem, makes a difference to the overall organization.

I would like to finish this chapter on empowerment with a story of a telephone operator who, by example, makes an invaluable contribution at one of Australia's largest appliance manufacturers, Email. And although this incident occurred about 10 years ago, before the term "e-mail" became part of our popular vocabulary, the message is equally relevant for today.

I owned a very old refrigerator that constantly leaked on the floor. When I telephoned to book a service call, the operator politely recorded the necessary details and booked a service call for the following week. As she was about to hang up, something prompted her to say: "I used to have a fridge like that with a similar problem. Rather than stay home and wait for the service call, you may wish to take a bit of pipe cleaner and see if there is a blockage in a U joint in the little tray that runs along the top of the fridge."

She patiently explained the procedure and, sure enough, there was no more water leak on the floor; and I'd saved myself $70 for a service call. I was delighted and recalled the story a few days later, citing this telephone operator as an example of how someone genuinely cared about a customer problem and was willing to do that little bit extra, although it wasn't "their" job. I was astounded when colleagues responded they wouldn't want that sort of person in their organization because she had "cost" Email $70 on a service call. I maintained that the customer brand loyalty she had engendered was worth more than $70. Furthermore, the word-of-mouth advertising gained by the amount of people I've told would be worth thousands to the company in advertising dollars alone.

A few months later, I realized I'd never taken time to let Email know how pleased I was with their service. I also felt guilty for not obtaining the telephone operator's name so I could have management personally thank her. So, belatedly, I wrote a letter to Email thanking them in broad terms. A few days later I received a phone call and met their executive general manager of customer service. I was astounded to learn that they receive more than 3,000 phone calls on a Monday alone. And, an operator took that extra minute out of a hectic schedule to help me with my problem.

I was even more amazed to walk into a room with about 30 receptionists with headsets and see my letter pinned to the wall. A few of them applauded when I was introduced. This was both embarrassing and amusing until I realized the significance that a brief "thank you" letter had to those staff. You see, they are the behind-the-scenes people who are vital in the Email customer service relay chain. But generally, the only time they will ever hear from a customer is if something goes wrong, even though the telephone operator would not have been at fault.

A receptionist plays a vital role in an organization, which has a number of strategies in place to make everyone feel part of their customer service team. That Email receptionist epitomized the right attitude; the attitude that goes far beyond doing one's job. And as one of them told me: "At parties I always introduce myself as the Director of First Impressions, which really makes people think!" she laughed.

It's important that we do think about how our customers are thinking and keep our sense of humor at all times in service provider roles (we need it!). I love a sign at a Surfer's Paradise food outlet, located on a main highway, which reads: "Stop and eat so we both don't starve."

They have a sense of humor and know that even when customers might be ill-humored, they still pay our salary!

I don't know the origin of the following excerpt as I've had it since I was at high school but it certainly sums up this chapter on empowerment:

That's not my job

There is a story about four people named Everybody, Somebody, Anybody, and Nobody. There was an important job to be done and Everybody was sure that Somebody would do it. Anybody could have done it but Nobody did it. Somebody got angry about that because it was Everybody's job. Everybody thought Anybody could do it but Nobody realized that Everybody wouldn't do it. It ended up that Everybody blamed Somebody when Nobody did what Anybody could have done.

—Anonymous

SEVEN KEY POINTS
in this chapter on empowerment:

1   Eliminate unnecessary bureaucracy to make employees more responsible and response-able.

2   Look at creative ways to say yes to customer problems, rather than "cop outs" to say no.

3   Encourage sensible risk-taking and learning from mistakes.

4   Support employees and catch people doing things right.

5   Recognize and reward employees for a job well done. Say "thank you" more often.

6   Make everyone feel important on the customer team, whether serving internal or external customers.

7   In my own organization, I will improve service through empowerment by:

_____

_____

_____

_____

_____

_____

_____

CONCLUSION

Service is a journey—not a destination.

There is no conclusion to customer service. There is only a beginning. There is no finish line but, like any championship relay team, it's crucial to burst out of those starting blocks as soon as possible.

Quality service is a journey not a destination. Like any journey, it starts with the first step. It's not easy. Go back and reread the sections in this book that you have highlighted and write down something from the seven chapters of the S.E.R.V.I.C.E. acronym, that you can implement within the next seven days to improve service levels within your own organization.

If I waited until I had collated all the service standards and stories I've heard into examples in this book I'd never finish it and, what's more, it would read like War and Peace, Part Two. At one stage, I was more surprised than anyone that this book was the number-one best-selling business book in Australia but I know there's always room for improvement, so naturally I welcome any reader feedback for future editions. If your organization believes you can simply continue to do things the way you've always done them, the competition will catch up, regardless of how good you may be.

As former Australian Prime Minister Malcolm Fraser once said: "Life wasn't meant to be easy." Neither is service. But service, like life, is what you make of it. Service is a lot easier to talk about than it is to implement on a daily basis. I know this to be true because I know my staff will be reading this book and thinking to themselves: "She doesn't always do this or that."

I'm far from the perfect manager but I honestly try to implement most of the strategies I've talked about in this book, bearing in mind that I'm a small business. Customer service is often the first thing talked about and the last thing done. Make sure it's one of the first things that is done when you finish reading this book. However, it's unrealistic to believe anyone can embrace all the strategies outlined in this, or other, books—so set priorities.

Do read what has worked elsewhere and evaluate which aspects will work for you. Reject the others. Don't expect an overnight turn-around-unless you also believe in the tooth fairy!

- Quality service cannot be seen as a program that comes and goes. It cannot be regarded as the flavor of the month, but must be seen as an integral part of everyday business life.
- Service is people. It is a partnership with employers, employees, suppliers, unions, and professional associations.
- Develop your own strategies to add value and make a difference to the future of your company and your country.
- If you come up with just one idea that you can, and will, implement, your investment in this book has been worthwhile and so has my investment of time.

There will always be new things to learn as new standards are set. Englishman Roger Bannister was seen as a miracle man when he broke the four-minute mile just a few days before Australia's John Landy did likewise. So too with global competition in service excellence. Now, top high-school athletes can break the four-minute mile. Athletic and service benchmarks have changed and will continue to change.

The Olympics, whether you're fortunate enough to attend live, as I've been, or watch on television, symbolize athletic excellence-excellence that is only separated by a fractional difference, a second here or there. So too with service; it's the little tiny differences that make the big difference.

Canadian by birth, educated in the United States, employed in Japan and Hong Kong, I realize the increasing global nature of sport and business. I was thrilled and honored to carry the Olympic torch on the day of the opening ceremonies of the Sydney 2000 Olympics, to play a small part in something much bigger than myself. And, all of us, wherever we live, whatever we do, must all strive to be internationally competitive and attain world-class excellence by carrying the flame, the passion, for customer service. By doing so, we serve not only our customers—but our community, our country and our planet.

To those committed to improving service quality, no further explanation is necessary. To those who aren't, none is possible.

As my wise father once said:

Let's turn common sense into common practice!

We sincerely hope that you have found the words in this book both timely and timeless. If you would like Catherine to customize a presentation for your next conference, please send an e-mail to **office@greatmotivation.com** or contact our Web site **www.greatmotivation.com**

REFERENCES

Albrecht, Karl, and Lawrence Bradford. *The Service Advantage.* New York: Dow Jones, 1990.

Albrecht, Karl, and Ron Zemke. *Service America.* New York: Dow Jones, 1985.

AMR: Quantum Report, "Customer Satisfaction Australia." March 1993.

Australian Bureau of Statistics. Household Expenditure Survey: Details Expenditure Items, 1993-94. Cat. No. 6535.0.

Barker, Joel. *discovering the Future.* St. Paul, Minn.: ILI Press, 1989.

Berry, Leonard, David Bennett, and Carter Brown, *Service Quality.* New York: Dow Jones, 1989.

Blanchard, Ken. *The One Minute Manager.* United Kingdom: Willow Books,1983.

———. *Legendary Service.* www.kenblanchard.com

Campanella, Jack. *Principles of Quality Costs.* 3d ed. Milwaukee WI: American Society for Quality (ASQ) Press, 1999

Carlzon, Jan. *Moments of Truth.* Ballinger, 1987.

Civil Aviation Authority of Australia. www.casa.gov.au.

Cruzatta, Miguel. *Reader's Digest.*

Davidow, William, and Bro Uttal. *Total Customer Service.* New York: Harper & Row, 1989.

Forrest, Philip. *Sold on Service.* United Kingdom: Carlson Marketing, 1987.

Foster, Richard N. *innovation—The Attacker's Advantage.* London: Macmillan, 1986.

Gates, Bill. *Business at the Speed of Thought,* United Kingdom: Viking, 1999.

Glenn, Peter. *It's Not My Department.* New York: William Morrow, 1990.

Guaspari, John. *The Customer Connection.* New York: AMACOM, 1988.

Health Insurance Commission. NHS Renumeration Per Prescription Data and 1991–92 Annual Report.

Horovitz, Jacques. *How to Win Customers.* London: Longman, 1990.

Huebsch, Monte. *Internetprofit.com.au.* Queensland: AussieWeb Pty Ltd., 1999.

Huey, John. "Nothing is Impossible." *Fortune,* 23 September 1991, 79.

Johnson, Daniel. *Flight Deck.* March 1990.

Karatsu, Hajime, and Ikeda Toyoki. *Mastering the Tools of QC.* Singapore: PHP Institute Inc., 1987.

Le Boeuf, Michael. *How to Win and Keep Customers.* New York: The Business Library, 1987.

Levitt, Theodore. "Marketing Success Through Differentiation—Of Anything." *Harvard Business Review* (Jan/Feb 1980): 85.

Mackay, Hugh. *Reinventing Australia.* Sydney: Angus & Robertson, 1993.

Moss Kanter, Rosabeth. *When Giants Learn to Dance.* New York: Simon & Schuster, 1989.

Naisbitt, John. *Megatrends.* New York: Warner Books, 1982.

Peters, Thomas J. "On Achieving Excellence." Newsletter. Peters, Thomas J. *Thriving on Chaos.* New York: Knopf, 1987.

Peters, Thomas J., and Robert H. Waterman. *In Search of Excellence.* New York: Harper & Row, 1982.

Zemke, Ron, and Dick Schaaf. *Service Edge.* New York: New American Library, 1989.

INDEX